Reflections of a

Child Bride

By Trudy Lynn

ISBN 0-7414-5053-4

Published by:

INFINITY
PUBLISHING.COM

1094 New DeHaven Street, Suite 100
West Conshohocken, PA 19428-2713
Info@buybooksontheweb.com
www.buybooksontheweb.com
Toll-free (877) BUY BOOK
Local Phone (610) 941-9999
Fax (610) 941-9959

Printed in the United States of America

Printed on Recycled Paper

Published January 2009

Acknowledgments

I would like to thank my friend, confidant, and collaborator, a man overflowing with talent and artistic ability.

Without you, this book would not have been possible. You turned a dream into a reality with your ability to capture my thoughts and interpret my feelings.

You are the person with whom I have felt safe enough to share my deepest, most intimate thoughts and emotions. I entrusted my life to you without fear of judgment or persecution, and you have supported me through this process of taking a walk though my life, both when it was painful and when it was humorous.

You have patiently waited and held my hand through the storms and waves of emotions that came during the pain of remembering. You have treated me with the utmost respect and dignity, allowing me to sit and absorb my thoughts and feelings until I could continue.

You never gave up on me, and made it possible for me to give hope to others who have been, or are, hurting in silence. You have helped me offer courage to them, that they may hang on until help arrives, and look forward, knowing there is a better way to live and the possibility of a peaceful future.

You have given me a voice.

I would also like to thank Kathy Grow for her tireless devotion to editing, re-editing, and re-re-editing this book. You, the reader, have her to thank for the chapter subtitles as well as the short, quick paragraphs which have made this book so much easier to read. Kathy was and is a true professional, and I am delighted to have had her help with preparing this book for publication. Thank you, Kathy, for everything you did to make this book special.

Trudy Lynn
July 2008

Contents

Introduction

A self-help book once opened with the words, "Life is hard." Yes, I know, a tired cliché.

But true.

Sometimes it is an exhausting struggle to stay one step ahead of the wave that threatens to crash down and envelop you.

There are people who have it good, going through life always able to ride the wave. I'm not suggesting they don't have to struggle, but either they were taught well or learned early how to stay balanced. They live happily, and fulfill their dreams and aspirations.

Others, like me, fight on a daily basis to ride the wave, just hoping it doesn't overtake them. And, when a big one comes and we go under, we find ourselves struggling for every breath, trying to stay alive, hoping we will soon rise to the surface. And you know what?

We always do.

Why I Wrote This Book

I am not a complainer, and I don't want this book to serve as a sad and morbid story of my travails and seemingly constant self-destructive behavior. Instead, I want this book to show people what they can overcome, if they only have the desire and will. I want people to know my struggles, and I want them to learn from, and not make, the mistakes I made.

This is not to say I'm not gaining from writing my story. In fact, in many ways, it has been cathartic for me to put down on paper some of the things that happened to me and how I dealt with them. I want my children and my parents and my other living relatives to get to know me and why I am the way I am. I especially want my children to forgive me (I hope) for some of the terrible things I did to myself . . . and to them.

For twenty years now, I have helped women who might otherwise have had no place to go and no person to whom to turn when they decided to make an about-face in their lives and find the inner strength to leave an abusive relationship and start the healing process. That process often takes years of distance in order to gain perspective, and it often takes professional help. In helping these women, I have helped myself; I have turned from a victim into a healer.

The Roots of Abuse

In that same vein, I have dedicated my life to helping people understand the roots of abuse.

When confronted with the story of a woman who refuses to leave her husband despite suffering emotional and physical abuse, many say, "Well, why doesn't she just leave?" or "That must be what she wants." To be blunt, it is not that simple.

The roots of abuse can often be traced back to childhood experiences with a trusted relative or someone who calls him/herself a friend. Women then sometimes stay in abusive relationships because of a general feeling of being trapped—of being caught in a hunter's snare, of struggling to free herself but seeing no option other than to chew her own leg off, wounding herself in the process of escaping.

Some women have few resources, either the emotional or material kind. Some do not have a reservoir of hope or the support of others; others feel love is worth fighting for, even if their spouses are abusive. Some lack the finances and/or education to move out and far enough away that abusers cannot find them.

Ultimately, however, fear keeps women in these relationships . . . fear of being alone . . . fear of not being able to take care of herself. It is the "deer caught in the headlights" syndrome. It is, quite simply, paralyzing.

And it is that paralysis that sometimes leads a woman to feel as if she has no way out other than suicide. And she tries. Once, twice, three times, maybe more.

Sadly, these attempts are sometimes successful. Even when they are not, the attempt itself is a cry for help, and one with ramifications far beyond the immediate need for "stabilization." Feelings of guilt spread like cancer, and no one is immune. The woman who made the attempt feels guilty for putting her family and friends through the psychological trauma. Family and friends feel guilty for thinking they may either have done something wrong or not done enough to help. And, like cancer, guilt feeds upon itself, growing and growing until chasms develop in relationships—chasms that seem irreparable.

But the cycle can be stopped. Things can be repaired, healed, mended. It's not easy and it often takes time, sometimes many years, but it can be done. It is POSSIBLE.

And that is true even more so today than it was thirty years ago when I went through the "cycle." Back then, especially in small-town Texas, "wife beating" was a taboo topic—a dirty little secret many families were afraid or unwilling to confront.

In those days, throughout the country—indeed, throughout most of the world—that was true, but, today, things have changed. The media now often document the lives of such women, and there are hundreds, if not thousands, of shelters and organizations with the sole mission of taking care of abused women and their children.

I feel blessed now to be part of such an organization, and I have pledged my life to help others—to make sure they KNOW there are people out there who have fallen below the wave, like they have, but who have found their way back to the surface.

The Persons We Want to Be

With each successive generation, we grow, we learn, we evolve. And, in the process, we find that our lives are like spinning wheels constantly gathering new threads and casting off the withered and old ones, leaving them behind as we march ever closer to being the persons we want to be.

I have not yet reached the point of complete satisfaction with who I am or what I am doing, and, frankly, I hope I never do. I hope I continue to learn, to grow, to adapt, to struggle, but to find joy where there is joy, to find a smile where there is laughter, and to find tears where there is sadness.

I decided a long time ago that I would not be a victim anymore. I have faced my worst nightmare—of being alone—and I am still here. I hope my story serves as an inspiration for all those women who struggle on a daily basis with the same issues I faced. Maybe it will not take them as long to reach the same conclusions I did. Maybe they will see the signs, and stay away from the type of men to whom I was drawn. Maybe, just maybe, they will find ways to stay ahead of the wave.

Prologue

For Better and For Worse

I remember a cold winter day when I was thirteen, one of those when you just want to stay in bed and read a book, or curl up in front of the fireplace or television. It was the kind of day you wouldn't think would be remembered for anything other than the cold weather—a perfectly forgettable day.

Instead, it was a day I shall never forget, for better and for worse.

My sister had been dating a man and we'd gone over to his house for dinner and to hang out. There was another man living there (and, although he was only twenty-two, to me at thirteen, he was a man), six feet tall, jet black hair, brown eyes. I had met Larry a few months earlier, and, even at my young age, I knew he was attractive, and the feeling was obviously mutual. He talked to me. He flattered me with kind words. He treated me like a princess. And I felt wonderful.

We had talked many times before this cold winter evening. He'd told me about his family and friends, his car, his job, his life. Then he had asked about my family, about my friends, about my life.

And I had told him. I had told him about my mother and father, and how they were strict but fair. I had told him about my grandmother, and how I liked to visit her and try on her fancy gloves. I had told him about my friends, and how we liked to chat on the phone, laugh at bad jokes, and make fun of certain teachers. I had told him about school, and how I wasn't doing that well, but still dreamed of becoming a teacher, pretending my animals, both real and stuffed, were students.

If Larry was anything, he was a sweet talker, and, the fact is, I was gullible. When he told me he loved me, I believed him. When he took me upstairs to his bedroom, I thought little of it. When he lay me down on the bed and started kissing me, I allowed it. Then, when he started touching me and groping me, then and only then did I begin to have a sense of overwhelming fear.

Wanting It to Be True

"It's okay, Trudy. This is normal for people who love each other, and I love you. I always will," he told me.

"Do you mean it?" was all I could muster. I so wanted it to be true. Part of me wanted to flee, but his words . . . his words were like an elixir making me feel special, wanted. Loved.

"Yes," he replied, with that damnably charming smile. "It'll be okay."

"But Larry . . . ?"

He put two fingers over my mouth as I protested. "Don't worry. It'll be over in a couple minutes."

And it was. In the moment, I didn't feel I had much of a choice. I tried to stop him, tried to wrestle free but he was bigger and stronger, and I . . . well, I just didn't have it in me to fight him. I had no idea of the consequences of what we had done. I just turned my head to the side, clenched my teeth in pain, and tried not to cry.

Why did I put myself in the position for what happened to happen? I can't say for sure. He told me he loved me and that he would love me forever. He told me he would treat me right. He told me a lot of things that night, most of which turned out not to be true. But I believed them because I wanted to believe them. I was thirteen. What did I know, except that it felt good to hear those things?

When he finished, he rolled over to his side of the bed and fell asleep while I lay frozen. What had happened? What had I just let him do to me? While he slept, my mind raced. Should I tell my mother? My father? Should I tell my sister? Anyone? Was what I had done wrong?

I didn't even know what the words "sex" or "intercourse" meant. Sure, I had seen pregnant women, but heck if I knew how they got that way. But there it was. I had done "IT" and didn't even know it.

Several weeks later, my mother asked me if I'd been having sex with Larry, took me to the doctor, and confirmed her and my father's worst nightmare. I was pregnant. Thirteen—a child myself—and having a child.

My Road, My Journey

I said that cold winter's day was one I shall never forget, for better and for worse, and I meant that.

For better? Because I love my son dearly. For worse? Because of what I put him and my daughter through during some very difficult years of struggling to overcome being a teenaged mother. One unforgettable winter's eve, and I was set on a path over which I felt I had no control. Through tough times, good times, tough and good times again, it's been a long road, one on which I continue to this day.

Yet, looking back, I cannot say whether, in the balance, that road was good or bad, right or wrong, black or white. Because it was my road! It was my journey!

It is my life!

Chapter 1

Square-Headed Dutch Girl

I was sitting on my grandfather's lap, playing with his chin, while he spoke to my grandmother in his deep-timbred voice, almost husky, but somehow soothing in its ancient-seeming tone of wisdom and kindness. Although I didn't know it at the time, here was a man who had lived through the Great Depression and dust bowl years, who had struggled on a daily basis just to survive. And that came through in his voice in a way I will never forget.

"I'll fix the chair in the living room in a little bit," he said. "Let me play with my square-headed Dutch girl of a granddaughter."

When he said that, I gave him a strange look. What did he mean? I had seen pictures of myself. As far as I could tell, I didn't have a square head. And no one ever told me I was Dutch. Was I? Now my mind was filled with images—the Dutch boy on a can of paint, one particular brand of shoes, a Shirley Temple movie, and, of course, cartoons.

Little did I know that my grandfather actually meant I was a hardheaded person, stubborn and cantankerous, given to crying fits until I got my way. At the time, not knowing what he meant, I took it as a term of endearment.

Then he smiled at me. "Give Papa a kiss," he said. And I leaned in, gave him a big smooch on the cheek, and settled into his strong arms, resting comfortably against his rising and falling chest.

For a long period, that was my identity. I was my grandfather's "square-headed Dutch girl." I was unique. I was special. I was Trudy Lynn.

The Oil Man and the Real Texas Lady

Born in Luling, Texas, on July 5, 1956, I was the younger of two daughters. My father was a big strong man, six feet tall, his

4

brown hair in a flattop, his eyes blue behind black-rimmed reflective glasses. He worked in the oil fields during the Texas boom times, earning a good living and taking care of his family. He was strict, often prone to fits of anger when provoked, but, mostly, he was—and still is—a good family man.

And he had a wicked sense of humor.

As a child, I was always scared because he was missing part of his thumb. And when I say missing, I mean gone, cut off, nothing but a stump from the knuckle up. When I sucked my thumb (which I often did) while my father read the paper, he would occasionally notice. Lowering the paper and looking at me with those steely eyes, he would say, "Trudy?" I would look up eagerly and he'd hold up his stump. "See this?" I would nod, hanging on his every word. "You know how I lost it?" I shook my head, even though he had told me the same story a hundred times before. He would continue to stare at me, his gaze deadly serious. "I lost it sucking my thumb," he said in a deadpan voice. Then he would glance at his stump and return to his paper, leaving me stupefied as I ripped my thumb from my mouth and pledged never to suck it again.

While my father was an oil man, my mother was a real Texas lady. Polite, refined, pretty, with light green eyes and light-colored hair, she always wore red lipstick and never left the house without being made up and dressed properly in high heels (and I mean high!) and stockings. And a girdle. Proper. Texan.

She used to come to school and all the kids would marvel at her, how pretty she was, and how she had such a nice smile. I was so proud and so happy to have such a "special" mother.

Yes, she was proper and always well-mannered. But she could also be ruthless when necessary—for example, when I was five and the neighbor's German Shepherd attacked me, and she told the dog's owner to lock the dog up or she'd shoot it. Like I said. A real Texas lady.

She was also quite nurturing and loving. I remember her hosting Tupperware parties when I was about five. I would peer around the corner into the living room and just listen in sheer wonderment as all those nicely dressed ladies talked and ate and talked. (My mother actually did very little selling.) One time, I went into the kitchen and sneaked a jelly doughnut. Although she never said anything, I think my mother knew I was "stealing" a treat, but allowed my little thievery to go unnoticed.

5

As far as I could tell, my parents were madly in love with each other, always stealing kisses when they were "alone," always looking at each other with loving eyes, always caring for and helping each other. They didn't fight too often, and, even when they did, they always made up in short course.

One time, I even caught them dancing in the living room. Dancing! I was so embarrassed, I ran upstairs. My father came after me. "Trudy? Are you all right?"

I looked at him, even as I turned red, and nodded.

"You're not upset?"

I shook my head as I drew my knees up to my chest, trying not to smile.

He looked at me with questioning eyes. "You sure?"

Again I nodded.

"Okay," he said, then smiled and left to go back downstairs. Probably to dance some more!

Disney vs. Church

So my parents were madly in love with each other, my father made a good living, but, most importantly, they were good Christian folk. At least that was always the most important thing in my mother's eyes. I was raised to believe in God and Jesus and the Christian way of life. Church was a three-times-a-week event—Sunday morning, Sunday night, Wednesday evening.

I didn't mind it, or, at least, I didn't mind it when *The Wonderful World of Disney* wasn't on.

Mickey Mouse, Tinker Bell, the sparkling wand—that was the true Magic Kingdom, at least in my child's mind. When it was on, I'd put up a fight before leaving home, even though our television was a big old black-and-white set with knobs and dials and a rabbit-ear antenna. (When reception was poor, my father would send me outside to turn the big house antenna in a different direction.) When Disney came on, fuzzy or not, I didn't want to miss a minute of "magical" television and the chance to go wherever the producers wanted to take me.

When it was time to go to church, my mother would stand over me, all dressed up with a hat and gloves, and say, "We're leaving now."

I would look at her, my eyes tearing up, and she would give me a stern look—the kind that said, "Not tonight, Trudy. I'm not dealing with your tears. Now, let's go"—and, invariably, I would pout.

"But I don't want to go. I want to watch Disney." And then I would cry, as if maybe, just maybe, if I did, I would get my way. Tears would be streaming down my face and I'd be holding on tightly to my little baby doll, but my mother would have none of it. She would grab my hand and drag me outside, and, even as I crossed my arms, angry, resentful, she would smile and say, "That's no way for a young lady to behave. Now wipe your eyes, and let's get moving. We're going to be late."

At times, I hated church, if only because it took me away from Disney. But I loved the church people, friendly, warm, always dressed in their "Sunday best." I always felt part of something special when I was there, even if I would rather have been in front of the television. I would sit staring at the beautiful stained glass windows, my body aching from the hard wooden Puritanical pews, and play with my little baby doll while the preacher breathed fire and brimstone. And when I say "fire and brimstone," I mean it: "Sin, sin, sin. Hell, hell, hell." Those were the words which always stung.

By that time, I was too old for the "cry room," so named because it had two rocking chairs, a changing table, and a big glass window and speaker setup so the ladies could watch and hear the preacher.

In church, my mother would try to keep me quiet by giving me a half stick of Juicy Fruit, but that never really did the trick. So I would lie on my mother's lap while she stroked my hair and I played with my baby doll, laying her on the pew beside me, covering her with a little blanket a woman in church had given me.

I still have that little blanket. Maybe it was because the woman was so nice, so gentle, so calm and peaceful. I can still remember her big brown eyes, wide open, as she smiled and offered it to me one day. "Here you go, dear," she said. "A present for your little baby doll."

I thanked her kindly, then turned away and smiled. As I said, the people were so very nice.

Small-Town Texas

That was small-town Texas, though. When we lived in Luling, near my grandparents, then in Kenedy, and then Victoria,

7

it was the same. The neighbors all knew each other, and there was always something being exchanged—food, clothing, other kind gestures.

Our house in Kenedy was on Graham Road, in a quiet part of town. Situated on about half an acre of land, there was plenty of room for me to run free and play. And I took full advantage of it.

Riding a bike was my favorite activity. I used to ride and ride and ride, all day long if I could. Up the driveway, down the driveway, up the driveway, down again. I never got bored. And if I found myself tending that way, I'd figure out how to liven it up—like trying to grab peaches from our neighbor's tree as I rode by. That was a dangerous game, however, since my neighbor used to shout, "Those peaches are for cannin', not for eatin'."

My sister used to ride with me sometimes. I don't think she enjoyed it as much as I did, but, nevertheless, she would join me and we would find ways to make it interesting.

I remember one summer day in particular. Hot as Hades it was and neither of us wanted to stay outside too long, but, in those days, you were told to go outside and play until it was time to eat or you were called in. Not much of a choice there. "If y'all can't find something to do, I'll give you something to do," my mother told us. Of course, that meant chores, and neither one of us was interested in doing chores, so I put on my blue shorts and perfectly ironed white cotton blouse, and, barefoot (as we always were in the summer), we picked up our bikes and headed toward the street.

Before I knew it, my sister hollered, "Look, I can ride with my eyes closed." I stopped riding to turn and watch in growing horror as she veered one way, then another, then finally right toward me. I tried to get out of the way, but it was too late. She crashed into the back of my bike, sending me flying onto the driveway. Not a single scratch on her, but I was dripping blood from above my eye.

Crying, I ran into the house, calling for my father. "Daddy! Daddy! I'm . . . I'm . . . bleeding," I cried between sobs.

He came running, and, after what was probably an initial shock, he wiped away the blood. "It's not so bad," he said as he took from the medicine cabinet the "monkey blood" (the Southern name for Mercurochrome). He soaked a cotton ball in the red stuff, then started dabbing the wound. And it stung. I started jumping up and down on either leg, uncontrollably crying my eyes out. "Blow, Daddy, blow!" I screamed as he blew on the wound.

And, slowly, the blood stopped flowing and the stinging subsided.

"All better," he said. Then he gave me a hug and smiled. "Now go ahead and get back to playing." And, suddenly, everything was fine. I ran out and played, all better, just as my daddy had said. However, I never let my sister forget that she was responsible for my having a scar on my right eyebrow.

I have many other happy childhood memories—running around with my sister at the drive-in movie theater . . . sitting in the back of an old Chevy Corvair, with teacups and trays, playing "tea party" . . . the smell of home cookin' in the neighborhood on summer evenings . . . BBQ—Texas style! . . . Easter egg hunts on the lawn . . . Christmases full of joy and good cheer, even though, one time, when "Santa" came to the door, I was so scared, I held onto my mother's leg, as he kept asking me what I wanted for Christmas. Imagine that. A child afraid of Santa!

And there was the bowling alley. My parents used to bowl in a league, and, every Friday night, my father would gather us in the car and whisk us off to the alley. Smoky, but filled with laughter and, of course, some cussin' and carrying on, it was a child's dream. I would run around with a "sodie water" in one hand, a hot dog in the other, smiling at all the adults and basking in their comments—"Oh, how cute she is" . . . "What a lovely little firecracker."

Of course, when league was over, my parents HAD to let us try our hands at bowling. I would stand there in my socks, the ball almost as big as my head, as my father stood to the side, making sure I didn't drop it. I would take a couple of steps, then heave the ball. Landing with a thud, it would roll, slowly, so slowly, rumbling as it moved invariably toward the gutter. But I was happy just to have been given the chance.

All in all, as I said, I had a pretty happy childhood. And why shouldn't I have? Oil had made my family comfortable, and things were good. It was the late 1950s, early 1960s, the time of Kennedy, Camelot, the American Dream. If anybody was living it, we were.

Trouble at Home

But all was not as it seemed. By the time I was seven, we were living in Victoria, and I was becoming aware of my family situation. I was becoming aware of my sister's apparently incessant rage, and my parents' inability to deal with her. Every day seemed to bring some new problem.

It started with my sister just talking back. My mother would yell at her, and she would shut up. But then it grew more intense, more angry. And my mother would yell at her some more. Then my sister started having tantrums and throwing things across the room. Chairs, books, whatever. And my father would step in. Folding his belt in half, he would snap it back and forth, back and forth, in ritual fashion, scaring the bejesus out of us.

This is what happened when we "misbehaved," i.e., didn't listen to our mother. "I'm going to come in there and whip you if you don't mind your mother," he would say. Then, when we failed to heed his warning (which was often), he would enter the room and lean back slightly with his hand hooked lightly on his belt buckle as some sort of omen of what might come. Then, and only then, would he rush across the room with a wild look in his eye, half feigning fury, half filled with the real thing, yelling, "I'm going to whip you girls!" (Never "spank," always "whip.")

We would quickly stop whatever we were doing and behave when he started to unbuckle his belt. Neither of us wanted to get "whipped." Then he'd give his last warning: "If I have to come back in here again, I'm going to whip you." If we dared push him, he would be there in a flash, pulling out his belt in one motion. I can still hear the snap, snap, snap of the folded belt as we begged for our lives. And I thought belts were for holding up pants!

Mostly it was my sister who misbehaved, and he would chase her throughout the house. "Please don't hit me. I'll be good! I promise!" she cried, even as she threw things in his way to prevent him from getting to her. But he would always catch her eventually, and, when he did, would give her the promised whippin'.

I would watch in horror as these events unfolded, and then run outside or up to my room to hide, holding my hands over my ears, chanting *lalalalalalalalalalalala* as my parents and sister had it out.

One time, we were getting ready to eat supper. Chicken-fried steak and mashed potatoes, one of my favorites. I stood outside the kitchen, peeking in every few minutes to see if my mother was going to make creamed gravy. I used to spread it all over my plate and sop it up with a piece of bread. Yum!

Then, suddenly, out of nowhere, a bloodcurdling scream, and all hell broke loose. My mother screamed. My father screamed. "I hate liars. I can't stand liars," my mother cried. Then I heard the snap, snap, snap of the belt as my father got involved. Then furniture crashing to the ground. "Please, please," my sister begged. "I'm not lying. I'm not." More screams. More furniture crashing as my sister tried to get away from the snap, snap, snap.

I ran upstairs to my playroom, hid in a corner, and cried my eyes out, but I wasn't far enough away to drown out the screaming. So I did something I was never supposed to do. I opened the attic door. It was the only place I could think of to hide away. I climbed up into the dark, dusty, scary room, lined with black felt, the rafters exposed, and found a place in the farthest corner. Even there I could hear the screaming, so I placed my hands over my ears and started singing out loud, "Jesus loves me, this I know, for the Bible tells me so," over and over and over again until the episode was done. Then I climbed back down and returned to my room, nobody the wiser.

To Get Better

I hoped. I prayed. I pleaded with God for it to get better, but it never did. It just got worse. And I was caught in the middle. "See," my mother would say when my sister would act out and I would cry as the yelling increased, "see, you've made Trudy upset." Then later, when my parents weren't around, my sister would hit me. For no apparent reason, she would hit me. Once, twice, three times, sometimes more. When we were watching television, when we were outside, when we went to sleep at night . . . didn't matter. No reason. She would just hit me. And I couldn't tell my parents because they would again yell at her.

So I curled up with my constant companion, my "pipi"—a white satin pillow like the kind a ring bearer might carry down the aisle—and cried and cried and cried some more, until there were no tears left.

Eventually, my parents did something completely anathema to them: they admitted they couldn't handle my sister and sent her to counseling.

My father refused to go. I don't think it was his idea. In fact, I think the mere thought that my sister needed help from someone other than her family was crippling.

I remember the nights my mother and sister would leave and come back late. "Where did you go?" I would ask. "To get better," my mother would always reply, and I would not really understand, but I would still shrug my shoulders and say, "Okay," as if I did, and walk away.

But my sister did not get better. Not for a while at least. She was a rager. She continued to hit me for no reason, whenever she felt like it, and she continued to act out with my parents. I wanted so badly for her again to be the sweet and nice sister who would take me to a movie or wash my hair. Instead, she was a monster out of some horror movie, tormenting me at every turn.

Maybe that's not fair. She wasn't, and isn't, evil. She was a child, like me, and hurting in her own way, with no other outlet for her rage and frustration. Though she hurt me terribly, I cannot fault her, for she knew nothing else.

And so I retreated into a fantasy world—a world I created—a world of happiness, a world of joy.

My Other World

For as long as I can remember, I wanted to be a teacher. I used to have dreams about it as a child, and, when we moved to Victoria and I had my own playroom, I made sure to set it up as a school.

Up front was the big green chalkboard (a Christmas gift), and two or three boxes of heavy white chalk. I had lots of pencils, crayons, construction paper, paste, and, of course, a good pair of scissors. I had a big black Magic Marker (which, of course, I would sniff every once in a while!). Books, hand-drawn pictures, and the alphabet I had snatched from the cover of an old Big Chief tablet lined the walls. This was my castle. This was the place I could live out my dreams.

I would play with friends when they were over, pretending to teach them to read, giving them "lessons," otherwise playing the role of teacher. And when my friends weren't there? I would line up my pets, any and all of them, depending on the year. There was our dog Spot and, later, Barney, and our cats, Star and Rum, and occasionally a parakeet or canary (although I didn't bring them upstairs). They substituted nicely for real people, and, when they tried to get away, I would sit them right back down, disciplining them as any teacher would. "Now, I told you to sit and listen like a good boy," I would say. I don't think the animals liked me very much for that, but, all in all, they were good playmates.

I always started each session with the Pledge of Allegiance, and, when that was over, I would lead the "school prayer," pretending to be the principal talking into a microphone to the students over an "intercom" (nothing more than a box covered in black construction paper that I had hung on the wall). And when the "kids" were being naughty, I would pretend to call them to the office. THAT was fun.

I had many other interests as a child, especially music, although I never really had a chance to explore it. Our church did not "believe" in music, or at least they didn't have any instruments. (I guess making "joyful noise unto the Lord" didn't include musical instruments.) Whether that was a conscious choice or a matter of economics, I am not absolutely sure. However, when at one point my mother went back to work in a beauty shop and was too tired to take us to church, I started going with the Baptist neighbors across the street.

The first time I went into that church, I went wild with excitement when I saw the piano and organ. And heard people singing! I returned home, excited and out of breath. "Mama, Mama, you're not going to believe what they have at church!" She took my hand and smiled. "I know. I know. They have a piano and organ." I nodded excitedly. "Yeah. And people sit in the front and sing! They sing!" Again my mother smiled. "It's called a choir," she told me, and then I released myself from her hand and ran around the house, carrying my baby doll and chanting, "The church has a choir! The church has a choir!"

Sports were also something I always enjoyed, and, in fact, I was good at them. Dodge ball and kickball were my favorites, and, when we played at school, I was almost always the first one picked. I can still smell the big red rubber ball and hear the hollow vibrating sound as I kicked it. And, in my mind, whether true or not, I always kicked it over all the other kids' heads!

School Days

But school was not especially fun for me. At best, I was an average or below-average student. It was not that I was dumb; it was just that I learned more slowly than most of the other children. I understood everything, but it took me a while longer. Frankly, all

I think I needed was a little extra attention, but, in those days, if you didn't keep up, there was no one to help you get back to speed. So, while everyone else seemed to be moving forward, I felt stuck.

I did have some good teachers, though. I reserve my fondest memories for Mrs. Wells, my first-grade teacher. At the beginning of the year, we chose towels for our naps. Then, every day of the week, when it came time, we would lie down and sleep. Often Mrs. Wells would give me a quick hug or just a word of encouragement, and sometimes she would even stroke my hair like my mother did. When nap time was over, I would pretend still to be asleep because I did not want it to end.

As time went on and I moved up in grades, my troubles grew. I could say that it was because I was having a difficult time at home, but that's not entirely fair, as I struggled with other things as well.

I was having not just academic but also social problems. Although I was a part of the "in crowd," I never felt as good or as special as some of the other people in my "clique." The children of doctors and lawyers, they were destined for Ivy League schools and to make a lot of money. Me? I was the daughter of an oil worker and a beautician. College? What was that? My parents had never even mentioned it as a remote possibility. They thought (or so it seemed) I was going to get married and have children, or go to beauty school and become a hairdresser. Something like that.

So I never quite felt as if I belonged in this group, and I never quite felt my parents had the confidence that I could do whatever I wanted.

Thus, the news came as no real surprise one day when I heard my mother and father whispering in the dining room. I went upstairs to my room to play, but, just a few minutes later, my parents called me back down. They had serious expressions on their faces. "Trudy," my mother began, "I am sorry but you are going to have to repeat this year at school." I looked at them, unable to realize the true impact of what she was saying except that I felt like a failure.

When I look back, all I can remember is always feeling very alone, even before the problems with my sister surfaced. My first nightmares came when I was five or six. Frankenstein movies were very popular then, and I often dreamed about the monster chasing my family and me.

Only later did I realize how these feelings of loneliness contributed to my problems. But, as a kid, what did I know? I certainly trusted a great many untrustworthy people. Maybe it was my fault after all; I made the choices. Could I have made better decisions? In the end, I did, but, when I was younger, I learned very quickly how to make myself feel better—by getting the attention of men.

Chapter 2

Loss of Innocence

When I was a little girl, my family often traveled to Luling to see both sets of grandparents. On my mother's side, that meant visiting "Biggy" (her real name was Dorothy), a real Texas character.

Big in name and big in spirit, she was a dominant force in my life. Biggy used to wear large, gold, studded earrings and flashy rings. And an apron all the time, so she could wipe her hands. She was always doing something—cleaning, cooking, fussing. "Hungry?" she would ask as I followed her around. I would nod, and, in no time, she would fry something up for me.

Then there were the bubble baths in the big claw-foot tub in the bathroom. Cleanliness was important to Biggy. So was looking pretty. She was always washing me and dressing me up. Once a bubble bath was done, I would get out of the tub, dry off, and get into her "powder box," puffing powder all over my face and body and, of course, all over the floor, while her canary whistled in its cage.

Then she would let me play in her bedroom, dabbing perfume behind my ears, looking at all her fine hosiery and church gloves. I used to try on the gloves and "pretend" I was a lady, prancing around like I had somewhere important to go. What would have made it perfect is if Biggy would have let me try on her church hats, but those were off-limits.

The Place

She and my grandfather owned a business they called "The Café" or "The Place." It was a down-home, Texas-style, no-holds-barred joint where the beer was served cold and the food was as awful as anything one could imagine.

When I was with my grandmother, I often played there—not really a place for a child, but there I was. It was a cold place, both literally and figuratively. Even in the middle of the summer, the concrete floor was freezing to the touch. Battered old wooden chairs and cheap tables with Formica tops lined the floor. The bar also had a Formica finish, the barstools were covered in black vinyl, and there was no "ambience" save for flashing beer signs.

And the food! Today it would be considered deadly. Chicken-fried steak piled with white gravy, cheeseburgers, and grease-ridden French fries—heart attack on a plate.

Yes, the joint was a down-home dive, country bar. Serve 'em up and take their money was the unofficial motto.

Biggy would have nickels painted red for use in the jukebox. When there was no music playing (and by music, I mean country music—there is no other kind!), my sister, cousins, and I would grab one of those nickels and play a song. I cannot remember what we picked, only that it would be loud.

I also remember sitting on a barstool and doing what any kid would do, turning round and round and round until I got dizzy. Even now, I can see and smell the ice cooler behind the bar, a big silver chest with a top that rolled up and down. Biggy kept the glasses in there so they'd be frosted and ready for filling up with beer.

Not to toot my own horn, but I was a cute little kid. A petite blonde, I always went to the beer joint dressed in nice clothes. My mother made sure of that. When my grandfather was still alive, I would sit on his lap while he drank and smoked. He rolled his own cigarettes, and, every time he licked the paper closed, he would get a piece of tobacco in his mouth and spit it out onto the floor. I have this indelible memory of him sitting there holding a cigarette between his fingers while I watched the long trail of ash left as the paper burned away, until, finally, the ash fell to the floor.

"Biggy," he would say to my grandmother, "get our little gal a Coke, would you?" And my grandmother would bring one of those old-style thick glass Coke bottles; then I'd take some peanuts from the tray and put them in the bottle and watch the Coke fizzle before I drank it.

Old Men

But being cute was not necessarily a good thing in a beer joint filled with men getting drunk. The men in there were not the kind and gentle type, if you get my drift. They were crusty old men with half-grown beards, cowboy hats, and khaki pants tucked into worn-out boots, but, as a child, I thought they were wonderful.

The old men would call me over—"Hey, come sit on my lap"—and I sat on their laps and gave them hugs. As a reward, they gave me change out of their pockets. What an education! Give a man a hug and you get what you want. Later, it would be give a man a kiss, or give him sex, and you get what you want. It's all the same, really—pocket change, hundred dollar bills, diamond rings, or even a country club membership.

My sister, cousins, and I often went into the back of the bar where cases and cases of beer were stored in extremely strong waxed-cardboard boxes with handles. We climbed on them as if they were a mountain, and played on top. There was also a dolly one of us would stand on, while another pushed it around. It was like being on an amusement park ride.

I remember one time we did something which we knew was terrible —actually quite naughty and sinful for sure!—but we did it anyway: we snuck a peak into the men's room. I remember seeing urinals for the first time, and wondering how men could sit on such a thing! I also remember wondering why they had no toilets in there; the ladies' room had one! How did that all work? Not a lovely scene for a six- or seven-year-old girl.

There was always a man or two in the back of the joint, watching television or heading to the restroom. One time, when my aunt picked us up in the alley, we were running out when an old man said, "Come here and give me a hug goodbye." I ran over to him and gave him a great big hug.

My aunt, who had come in to see what was taking us so long, immediately intervened. She took me outside and scolded, "Don't you ever, ever, ever do that again."

"What did I do?" I asked. My aunt grew very stern, but, with compassion and a maternal protectiveness, said, "Hug one of those old men, those old sons of bitches. You never know what they're going to do." I looked at her loving, caring eyes and was puzzled. What could she mean? That hugging old men was wrong? I had hugged my grandfather many times. And I had been hugging other old men, too, in the beer joint. Should I not have been?

My aunt put her hand on my shoulder and leaned down so

her head was even with mine. "They could have a knife or something," she said. "You just don't know." (Circumnavigating her real concern, which was you should not let anyone "touch" you.) "Just don't let me see you doing that again," she finished, and we were off, with her now smiling warmly

The fact was, she was concerned and rightly so. I should never have been in that beer joint, let alone in the laps of men eight times older than I was.

For the first time in my life, I realized my aunt was different. She was trustworthy. She loved me. She was always looking out for my best interests. I used to fantasize about going to live with her and my cousins. She was just so nice and hardly ever yelled.

I wondered what it would be like to be growing up in that house with her and my cousins and my uncle. Would I have been giving these old men cheap thrills? Probably not. She always looked out for me, and, later in life, as I got into more and more trouble, she was still always there to talk to, to try to help. That was just the type of person she was.

The Portrait

My father's parents also lived in Luling and operated the only motel in town, one of those motor courts shaped like a U with parking spots in front of each room. I spent a lot of time there, too. The lobby was right inside the front door, and, behind the counter, a set of stairs led to where my grandparents lived.

Lots of oil workers stayed there; after all, Luling was in the middle of the big Texas oil fields. I remember when I was five or six, going with my grandmother to chop ice from the icebox for the patrons. I was always fascinated by how she was strong enough to cut off a big piece of ice with that little tool.

But things were not all fun and games in Luling. One summer day, my grandmother walked me down to one of the motel rooms. She had me in a white frilly dress with a single button in back and a sash tied into a bow. "You're going to have your portrait taken, dear," she said softly as she ushered me toward the door. I had no idea what she meant but it sounded fine to me.

Just as we got to the room, customers drove up. My grandmother told me she would go wait on them, and that I should return to the office when the man had finished "taking my portrait." She opened the door and I took the small wooden step and entered the room.

Immediately, the musty odor overtook me, the kind of dank smell that unused motel rooms get after a week or so—a combination of the Pine-Sol my grandmother cleaned with, the lack of air conditioning, and circulating dust. It was also extremely cold, and I immediately felt my arm and neck hairs stand on end. As the door closed behind me, I scanned the room, at first I thinking I was alone as my eyes adjusted to the low light.

A swag lamp hung over a small wooden table and two chairs. The bed was neatly made, a white chenille spread on top and the sheets, starched and crisp, pulled up under the pillow. On the other side of the room, there was a backdrop and two tall black poles with thick bulbs. Between the poles was a square rug about four feet by four feet, on top of which sat a small, six-inch-high table. Beyond that, through the open bathroom door, I could see the white shiny floor and sparkling bathtub.

A man was kneeling at the table, doing something with his camera. When he saw me, he smiled, warmly I thought, and motioned me to come in. I remember being very cautious. Not afraid, just cautious. He talked to me briefly as he continued to work the camera and I thought he seemed nice. Friendly.

When he was ready, he picked me up and set me on the table, and started taking pictures. Everything was innocent at first, as he gave me directions on where to set my eyes, how to hold my chin, where to put my hands. But then something happened. As he continued taking pictures, he began touching me more and more, first gently nudging me one way and the other, then moving his hands over my body. After that, everything got fuzzy.

Wrong

I can still feel his cold hands pulling my clothes off . . . the camera flashing as he used his big hands to angle me just right for the photos . . . feeling scared . . . wanting to scream but too afraid even to speak . . . praying my grandmother would come back . . . shivering in the cold . . . knowing that something was wrong, that this was wrong. I felt trapped, just like a caged animal, except that I couldn't move. I was paralyzed, detached, almost as if this were happening to someone else.

And then, somehow, I was in the bathroom. It was so cold, so very cold. I was naked and my feet were freezing on the tiled floor. I recall my dress being put on over my head, and the man's big hands trying to button the one tiny button. I was shaking the whole time, my body vibrating with fear.

He next led me back out to the main room, set me again on the little table, and took a few more pictures. And then it was over.

Of all the things I now remember about that hour, I most recall wondering what my grandmother had been thinking. Why had she taken me to that room? Didn't she suspect anything? I really do not know and I never asked her, although I cannot believe she did. She was the type of woman, who, if she had known, probably would have pulled out a shotgun and threatened in a very ladylike way to "take away his manhood" before the police arrived. At this point in my life, I think she just didn't know that type of thing went on and, since I didn't tell her, well . . . she never knew.

In fact, for a long time, no one knew besides me and the photographer. Maybe I should have told someone—my grandmother, my mother, my father. If I had, maybe I would not have ended up dealing with what I had to deal with later on. But I didn't, not out loud. In my mind, however, I could not imagine they didn't see a difference. How could they look at me and not see what had happened? My cries were silent, but I felt as if I were screaming out loud, trying to get someone's—anyone's— attention.

As an adult, I now realize that, unless you speak, people— including family members who do indeed care—don't always know what is going on. As a child, you think your parents are all-knowing and all-seeing. How could they not be? And, when you're five or six, you just don't question the people who love you. You don't ask your dad why he is so angry and flashing his belt. You don't realize that a beer joint is not a good place for children, especially when the old men there are using you for cheap thrills. You don't question your grandmother when she takes you into a room and leaves you alone. That is just how it is. And I never once imagined it could be any different. Maybe if I had, my life would have changed earlier, but that was not to be the case.

I never told a soul what happened that day. Nobody. Not until now.

My Father's Approval

The whole portrait episode actually seemed like a dream. Somehow, I had become disconnected from reality and couldn't even be sure it had happened. It was so shocking, I wondered if perhaps I had made it up. Perhaps I was going crazy.

Ironically, to say the least, I still have one of the "good" portraits from that day. My mother always hated it because she thought my grandmother had dressed me too old for my age. For some reason, though, I have kept it. Maybe it represents the loss of innocence. Sure, before that day, things weren't perfect, but they weren't terrible either. After that day, though, everything seemed darker, more terrifying. That time I left Luling feeling sick, and it wouldn't be until our summer camping trip a few weeks later that I returned to some sense of normalcy.

Often on summer break, my family would go to East Texas or Arkansas or Missouri to camp and fish. We used to go out in a little boat on the lake, just my father and I, and throw our lines in and, mostly, relax in the sun. He would hold his pole with one hand and drape his other arm over my shoulder, and I would snuggle up to him. We did not catch much, but that didn't matter. Those were among the few moments I remember of spending quality time alone with my dad.

I loved the water, and, when my father came home from a few days away in the field and said we were getting an aboveground swimming pool, I was ecstatic. I knew I was going to be the hit of the neighborhood, and, indeed, kids used to come from all over town to swim in our pool. I'd stay in the water for hours, splashing around, playing.

And I liked being the center of attention. I liked wearing my bikini despite my father telling me, "You shouldn't be showing yourself around like that." I liked that the boys looked at me, making me feel pretty and special.

My father made a lot of comments like the one about the bikini. He was always protective of me, but, paradoxically, he never really gave me a chance to show him what I could do. If I wasn't doing something he "approved of," then I was doing something wrong. I remember one incident quite vividly.

When I was ten or eleven, I was playing outside and noticed the grass was getting pretty high. So, I went into the garage, pulled the old green lawn mower from the corner, and started it up. I was having a good time mowing the lawn and minding my own business when my father came out the front door looking like he was ready to rage. He ran out, grabbed the lawn mower from my hands, and stopped the motor. "Girls don't have any business mowing the lawn!" he yelled.

He then took the mower, and, without finishing the job, put it back in the garage, leaving me standing there with tears in my eyes. He then came back and said, "Find something to do, young girl, and don't forget to make it ladylike."

I ran into the house crying and went straight to my playroom, my escape. I didn't like my father telling me what a girl could and couldn't do. I was independent: "I want to do it on my own," I always used to say when somebody tried to help me. "I can do it," I told my mother when tried to show me how to cut a potato. I was very obstinate that way; I had to learn and do for myself, always.

Refuge

But no matter my problems—whether they were with family, men, school, whatever—there was always one place I could turn for refuge. Church. Church was always a place of safety, comfort, security. When I was there, all my fears were relegated to the back of my mind. From fire and brimstone to the Baptist choir, I had found a place that felt comfortable, that felt like home. And I formulated some very concrete ideas about God in church, and about what it meant to be a good person and to be spiritual.

When I look back, I do not consider myself to have been "devout" when I was a child. I simply liked church and the friendliness of the people. But I really didn't understand much of what I was being taught. If I had to label myself back then, I guess I would say I was a "God-fearing Christian."

My mother and our preacher used to drum into us the part of the King James Bible that said, "The Lord will come as a thief in the night." Frankly, that scared me. To me, at six, it sounded like someone would come and steal little girls from their beds. So, I became frantically obsessive, having to say my bedtime prayer every night, so that, if I did die in my sleep, Jesus would take me. A copy of the "Now I lay me down to sleep . . ." prayer—the one every "good" Christian girl knows by heart by the time she's four—hung over my bed. And, since I wasn't "saved" until I was twenty, I was in constant fear, even in my teens, that I would be consigned to hell for eternity.

Later in life, I often wondered why God had allowed all the meanness and abuse I experienced. If Jesus had truly died on the cross to save us, why would he allow a man to beat his wife? Why would he allow her to be molested and raped as a child?

To this day, I have not come to a satisfactory conclusion. Maybe life is just one of those things during which you are supposed to learn as you go along. Maybe God is the "Clockmaker," winding the spring but allowing things to happen as they may.

I didn't know then and I don't know now, though I do have some ideas. At the time I was becoming a teenager, however, I only had a lot of questions and no answers, just I was about to go through what can only be described as my own personal crucible

Chapter 3

Crucible

It all began in the summer of '69—a strange summer, to say the least.

The summer of Woodstock and of more bad news in Vietnam, a year after Martin Luther King Jr. and Robert Kennedy were gunned down, it was a season full of contradictions, of renewed hope and of quiet desperation.

The big hit of the year was "The Age of Aquarius" from the Broadway musical, *Hair*. Were we entering a new age? Honestly, I don't know. In fact, I didn't know any of this at the time. In the summer of '69, I was a thirteen-year-old schoolgirl searching for my identity.

Summertime started innocently enough. I remember playing with my friends and sister . . . picnics and parties . . . church . . . getting inside to sit by the air conditioning when it got too hot, letting it blow on my face, my hair flowing back as I pressed closer.

One day in early August, my mother brought home a gift. Clothes! And not just any clothes, but a black bikini with pink polka dots. I loved it. Despite my father's comments to the effect that it wasn't "proper for a girl to be wearing such," I did anyway. Prancing around at the pool, in the backyard when it was hot, wherever and whenever I got the chance, I would wear it.

A few days later, I was at a pool party with a bunch of friends and some other people I didn't know. I was having a good time, splashing in the water, eating, showing off my new bikini. Getting out of the pool, drying myself off, out of the corner of my eye I noticed an older man looking at me. I guessed he was in his mid- to later twenties, and remember thinking he was very handsome, but definitely too old. Much too old. So I paid him no mind and went about the business of being a kid at a party. By the time I got into bed that night, I had forgotten the whole thing.

Back to School

The rest of the summer was uneventful and school started up in September as it always did. I never really liked school, never really liked how the teachers treated me or having to learn things I'd just as soon forget.

One day, my friends and I were sitting outside before the bell rang, and the same guy who had been staring at me a month earlier pulled up in his car, a Chevy Impala convertible. Very nice. Very well kept. He motioned to one of my friends. As she went up to the car, the rest of us started giggling. What were they talking about?

Then she turned and waved at us. "Come on," she said. "We're going to ditch school." The rest of us looked at each other. "Ditch?" we thought. "Can we?" After a couple of seconds, we shrugged, and, inside of a few minutes, we were in the car, on the road, driving fast.

As the car went by my mother's beauty shop, I ducked down on the floorboard, but, as soon as the car zoomed by, I was up again. The wind in our hair, the radio blasting, we were free for the day! We went to the park, played around. I really don't recall exactly what we did, except just enjoyed a day of ditching school.

I found out our driver was Larry. We talked a little. He was very engaging and seemed very interested in me, asking all sorts of questions about my family, my friends. And I was kind of awestruck. Here was this twenty-something man, handsome, strong, talking to me, interested in me.

He had tattoos on his forearm and upper arm. I no longer remember the one on the upper arm, but the one on his forearm was of a fancy cross, ornate and gold enough to be used in a papal ceremony. So, right then, I knew he was a good guy. After all, he must be a Christian.

I also remember how good he smelled. Whatever cologne he was wearing was intoxicating. Whenever I was near him, I leaned in ever so slightly (imperceptibly, I believed), and took a good long breath, savoring the wonderful fragrance. The scent of a man. Quite stimulating at any age.

But it was all innocent fun. I knew he was too old. So, when he drove us back to school at the end of the day, I figured once more that I would probably never see him again.

Well, there was another party at a friend's house. Just a bunch of kids having a good time, listening to music, laughing, telling bad jokes. And somehow Larry was there. I'm still not quite sure how he always managed to be around us younger kids.

This time, he came on to me. Tried to lean in when we were talking, to kiss my neck. I brushed him off with my hand and walked away. An older sister of one of my friends must have seen what had happened; after switching records, she came over to me. "Really listen to this song, okay, Trudy?" I nodded, and she smiled tightly and walked away.

Soon the stereo was blaring the Steve Lawrence tune, "Go Away, Little Girl." I half listened, half watched the other kids during the first part of the song, but, by the time the last stanza came on, I'd lost interest, instead finding two of my friends giggling about something and asking just what was going on.

In retrospect, I realize I probably should have paid more attention to the lyrics.

End of a Dream

I didn't see him again for another month. By November, my sister was dating a guy who, it happened, shared a house with Larry. She and I went over to their house to have dinner. Now, I had no intention of anything happening. Sure, I was curious about boys, curious about the possibility of kissing one, curious about all the fuss when my sister and her friends were talking about who was "making out" with whom. But, to me, that was the extent of my desire. Curiosity. Nothing more. I was in no rush.

At that point in my life, everything was just beginning, everything was in front of me. My dream was school, education, love, marriage, life, children, becoming a teacher, retirement, grandchildren, sitting on a rocking chair with my husband of forty years watching as the little ones ran around the yard with the three dogs and two cats all chasing them. That was my dream, and I knew it was going to come true, I just knew it. Because that is the way I wanted it.

But, as happens with life sometimes, fate took me around a different turn, a turn so dark that it engulfed a good portion of my life, a turn that would not only destroy my dreams for a time, but literally threaten to take my life as well.

So it's a cold day in November, and a cold night, in the low 30s. And snowing, at least in my memory, though I can recollect it snowing only four times in South Texas in all the years I've lived there.

So maybe this is wishful thinking, maybe just my way of gentling the edges of a terrible, fateful memory. But there it is. I can see in my mind's eye the soft, powdery flakes coming down, a few at a time, one here, one there, another over there. Against the backdrop of the darkening sky, it was quite beautiful.

I could see my breath as I exhaled, walking the length of the driveway, my heavy winter coat zippered up to my chin, my hands tucked into red mittens, my hat pulled down over my forehead, earmuffs and a scarf covering the rest of my exposed face. The house lay just up ahead, small but comfortable looking. I could see the warm, inviting light and couldn't wait to get inside, to throw off all my outerwear and maybe sit by the fire and drink a cup of hot cocoa. The four of us were going to have dinner. We'd all play games, we'd all laugh, and then we would go home. Simple. Fun.

And, for a while, it was exactly that. Fun, deliriously fun. Inside, Larry and my sister's boyfriend cordially helped us off with our coats. We all sat down in the kitchen, and, as Larry cooked, my sister and her boyfriend chatted while I listened, chiming in now and then, probably with some silly thirteen-year-old's comments but, heck, that's who I was.

When the meal was ready, Larry brought the food over and portioned it out. We were all famished and dug in quickly. It was—in a way that later seemed ironic—quite delightful. Larry, my sister, her boyfriend, everyone was friendly. We were talking, eating, laughing. I was smiling, enjoying myself, having a great old time.

Now my memory gets a little hazy. I don't recall the specifics, but what I do remember is that somehow Larry and I were left alone. I remember feeling uncomfortable, just as I had when in that musty motel room. I felt like a scared little girl. Was it just my imagination or were there warning signs? Maybe.

Whatever the case, there was really nowhere I could go. I couldn't walk home, not in that weather, so I stayed. And Larry and I talked. He was quite charming, telling me stories of things he had done, crazy things, stupid things, funny things. I remember laughing, especially when he smiled. He really was handsome. But still, even at this point, I knew I was only thirteen and this "man" was too old for me. Yet, when he asked me if I wanted to see the rest of the house, like any good girl, I knew my manners enough to say, "Yes, I'd love to," and headed on upstairs.

The Bedroom

He showed me quickly around the second floor, then took me to the last room at the end of the hall—his bedroom. He sat me on the bed, and, still talking, went into the bathroom, leaving the door open just enough so I could see what he was doing.

However, I tried not to look. In fact, I turned my entire body around and even went so far as to cover my ears so I would not have to see or hear what he was doing.

Then, suddenly, I smelled the scent of his cologne wafting in the air, and, when I turned, there he was standing before me, clean-shaven and wearing nothing but his underwear. Just his underwear! I had never seen any man with his shirt off, not even my father, and here Larry was standing before me with nothing between himself and nudity but a thin piece of white cotton.

That was when fear started to grip me, to hold me, to paralyze me. This wasn't right. Not at all. Not a chance. And, yet, what could I do? My gut told me to bolt. To run right out of the room, down the stairs, grab my coat, and flee out the door. But I didn't listen to my gut. Or I did, but I was just too paralyzed by fear to do anything about it.

As my nervousness grew, my hands started shaking and I tried to hold them together in front of me so he wouldn't notice as he walked around the bed and as he sat down next to me, his flat stomach curling just a bit over his belly button.

At first he just sat there, looking at me. I tried to look away. But he put his hand on my cheek and turned my head toward him. Slowly, he began caressing my hair, softly, gingerly, like a true lover.

And yet I knew. I knew! This was wrong. I shook even more, but, the more I tried to stop it, the more I felt myself shaking. As he looked at me, I tried to look down, but he put his hand under my chin and held my face at eye level to his. Then, leaning in, he started kissing me. First on the cheek, then moving to my lips.

I hate to admit this, but it felt nice. The kissing especially. So tender. So warm. His lips were soft and he was very gentle. Throughout, he was also hugging me, the scent of his cologne intensifying the effect.

And I was feeling that effect, of being a post-pubescent girl feeling the touch of a man. My mind was racing. This felt so nice. So good. But it was wrong! He was twenty-two! I was thirteen! What was happening? What was I doing? Yet, as my gut continued to churn, screaming its message that I should run, run, run and not look back, I remained where I was. And, before I knew it, it was too late.

The hugging stopped and he put his hands on my shoulders and gently lowered me to the bed, my bare neck brushing against the coarse blanket as my head fell to the pillow. He continued to kiss me, on my cheeks, on my lips. The pace of what was happening increased.

To this point, I had not resisted, not even offered any hint of a no, but now, as I felt his hand move onto my breast, then toward my waist, lifting up my shirt, I had had enough. "No, Larry," I said in as strong a voice as I could muster. Meek to be sure, but it was the best I could do. "Please, no."

He did not answer. Did not stop. Instead, he moved faster, lifting my shirt above my head, revealing my bare midriff and bra. "Larry, stop." I tried to yell, to scream, but I know it came out as merely a whisper. I began to struggle, tried to use what little strength I had to push against his chest, to push him off me. But he was too large, too strong, and my movements had little effect.

"Don't you love me?" he asked as he continued to intensify the pace, touching me, kissing me. "Don't you want me to love you?"

That last . . . that last thing he said. "Don't you want me to love you?" That hit me.

"Yes," I wanted to say, "But not like this. Not now." Instead, all I could say was, "I don't know, I don't know," all the while struggling to keep myself from crying.

I kept trying to push him off me, even as he reached down and unzipped my pants, pulling them down around my ankles. But he wouldn't budge. I lay there half-naked. It was so cold. So very cold. My mind was racing, filled with stupid things like, isn't the heat on? All the while, shivering, I was trying to push him off me.

"Don't you love me?" he asked again. "'Cause, if you do, then you'll do this," he said. "And if you don't, I'm going to run out of here and kill myself."

What? What did he say? Kill himself? Where did that

come from? What was happening? This wasn't real! This wasn't happening! But it was real. It was happening. And, soon, one hand reached behind my back and unhooked my bra as the other hand pulled my underwear down below my knees.

No!

"Come on, Trudy," he said. "You're going to like this. I promise."

I shook my head from side to side, scared of what was going to come next. He just smiled and reached up, forcing my arms down above my head.

"Please, no!" I cried, the tears running down my face. "Please, no!" I thrashed about with my legs, trying to kick him, trying to hurt him, trying to get him off me. But I couldn't. I had missed my chance to get away. Now the full weight of his body was on top of me. I was pinned. There was nothing I could do. Nothing at all. I began to cry uncontrollably.

Then I felt something warm touch me between my legs. I would have jumped up with all the force I could muster, but I couldn't. Instead, I was shocked back into reality. My mind raced. What was that? What was touching me? What is he doing? Suddenly, I realized, this is the dirty little secret my parents kept to themselves. This was sex! No!

I began to beg. "Larry, please! Please, let me go! Please! I don't want to do this!"

I continued to struggle, moving my body one way, then the other, pushing him upward with my arms, trying to shake my legs so he could not get inside me, trying to kick him, trying to scratch him, trying to scream. "Larry! Please! No! No!"

Meltdown

Then suddenly, he jumped off the bed. Naked, his face flushed, he faced me, screaming, shouting. "You want this!" he cried as he hit the wall with a karate chop. "I know you do!" He threw another hand at the closet door, which banged against the wall with a deep thud, then flew back. "Fucking shit!" he screamed as he picked things up from the closet—clothes, hangers, odds and ends—raising them above his head, then throwing them in one motion onto the floor. "Fucking shit!" he screamed again. "You know you want this. I know you want this."

The whole time he was having a meltdown, I remained

lying on the bed, half-naked, completely frozen. I could not think. I could not act. I had even stopped crying at this point. Shock had overcome me. I was completely paralyzed, thinking I was going to die, that Larry in his rage was going to pick up something and beat me to death.

This was the time to run. To run and never ever, ever look back. Larry was probably drunk, probably wouldn't have been able to make it down the stairs. All I had to do was take this first lunge toward the door. Screw the fact that I was naked. This was my life at stake. Run, run, run, my mind kept telling me. Run out the door. Somebody help me, please! Help!" That's all it would have taken. Someone would have come, would have seen what was happening, would have called the police, called my parents. Larry would have gone to jail. And I would have been safe. Scared, frightened, but safe.

All this went through my mind in a split second. That's all the time I had to act. But, instead of leaping up and running, I froze. I did nothing except wait while Larry continued his rampage, tearing the curtains off the windows, throwing them to the ground, stomping on them, his face more red with every action.

Then, I watched him slowly remember I was there. When he turned back to me, I remember thinking, "Oh, my God. What is going to happen next?" But I knew. I already knew what was going to happen. And it did. Repeatedly.

By that time I had given up. I was ready to die right there and then. I even prayed for death.

I looked out the window as Larry did what he did. I think it only took a few minutes, a few minutes during which I stepped outside myself—the only way I could protect my mind from the horror of what was happening.

I remember watching the few snowflakes falling outside the window. How beautiful they looked, their whiteness glistening against the backdrop of the night sky. I imagined myself one of them, meandering down until I hit the ground, then slowly melting, melting into the earth, spreading outward until I was no more.

As quickly as it had started, it was over. He rolled off me and to the other side of the bed, then closed his eyes and quickly fell asleep.

Going Home

How long I remained there, I don't know. A minute, two, three, ten, it doesn't matter. I lay there still naked, my body convulsing, feeling like all I wanted to do was vomit. Finally, I forced myself upward. In a daze, I pulled up my underwear and pants, put on my bra and shirt, and stumbled downstairs. I reached the living room, made sure my shoes were on, then sat looking at the television as if it somehow held the answers to what I should do next. But it did not speak to me. I simply stared at it in shock, unable to cry, unable to stand. Motionless. My mind had just switched off.

Again, the length of time does not matter. I sat there while Larry slept. Sat there for a good long time, hugging my knees, then finally left. There were no goodbyes.

As soon as I arrived home, I ran to my room—to my playhouse, to my animals, to the things I knew and loved, the things that had been taken away from me a short time before.

Not taken physically but emotionally. How could I ever recover from this experience? I curled up on my bed, my cat snuggled beside me. In the fetal position, I rocked, back and forth, back and forth, back and forth. The tears would not come. If they had, I'd probably have awakened everyone in the house. Instead, I rocked and rocked and rocked, until, finally, I fell asleep from sheer exhaustion.

The next morning I awoke, went downstairs, and had breakfast with my family. Nobody asked me anything.

I am in my fifties now, and I KNOW I should have told at least my mother or my aunt. Someone. Anyone who could have helped, who could have changed what was to come next.

But I didn't.

How could I? What would they have said? That it was my fault? That I had been stupid, going into a twenty-two-year-old man's room? Yes! I knew it now! But before? When it happened? How could I have known?

I should have cried out for help, and, maybe, in my own way, I did. But it never occurred to me that I could actually tell my family or anyone else. This kind of thing just did not happen. Ever. And rape? What was that? The word itself had no meaning to me. So I was the only one, the only one carrying my deep, dark secret. Nobody could help me.

Day in and day out, I kept the awful truth to myself.

Through dark and lonely nights, I pretended that it hadn't even happened. I blocked it out, hoping if I made myself forget even being in Larry's house that cold night, the whole thing would go away like some magic mist.

So, for the next few weeks, I went on with life. I went to school. I did my homework. I played with my friends.

And I kept seeing Larry.

Why? I really can't say. I was young. I was stupid. And I was desperate, feeling completely alone, isolated, trapped. Unable to express any of my feelings or fears or doubts to my parents, I shut them out completely. How could I have done otherwise? And I couldn't tell my sister either. What would she think of me? What would she do? Would she even care? So there I was, alone in the world, at thirteen.

And the only one who paid me any attention was Larry.

Chapter 4

Too Late

Larry came over one night a couple of weeks later. My parents let him in, and he came up to my room. There he sat down on the bed and offered me a "promise ring." He told me he was sorry for what had happened, that he loved me, that he had been drinking and that he was a fool. He told me again that he loved me.

And I believed him. I let him put the promise ring on my finger and we started kissing. Mere moments later, I felt his hands at my waist. Thankfully, my mom knocked on the door and Larry pulled back. "You guys need to keep the door open, okay?" my mother said. I smiled politely, as did Larry, and we both promised. My mother walked away, and we kept talking for a good hour or so before he left without any further incident.

After he left, my parents called me downstairs. They sat on either side of me on the couch. "Trudy dear, we know you've been seeing Larry and we want you to stop. He's too old for you, you understand?"

I didn't understand. In fact, I was angry. Who were they to tell me what to do? Who I could see and who I couldn't? I acted like the typical love-struck teenager, running out of the house, crying. Here I had found a man who'd given me a promise ring and had told me he loved me, and, despite what he had done, I'd fallen for him. And now my parents were telling me it was over? Because they wanted it to be?

I remember standing outside, shivering in the cold, crying. Then my father came out after me. "Trudy dear," he said softly, "we just want you to be happy, and we don't think Larry is right for you, you understand?"

I looked up at him, saw he was upset, and then something magical happened. He drew me into his arms and hugged me. Hugged me like he had never hugged me before.

Was that his way of trying to hold on to me? To stop me

from doing something that would ruin my life? Maybe. In retrospect, I wonder if maybe that hug was all he had.

My dad and I sat down and talked, and I told him how nice Larry was, how sweet and kind and generous, and, finally, he relented. "Okay, he can come to the house. But you can't see him anywhere else, all right?" I smiled and hugged my father again. I was so excited. I could still see Larry!

And I wanted to. After all, he had apologized for that night, told me he loved me, told me he was sorry, that he'd been drinking and was a fool. He told me it would never happen again. And I bought into it. Every last word.

Bad Bargain

A month went by, maybe two, and Larry and I continued to meet, and not just at my house. I wasn't holding up my end of the bargain with my father.

I had grown to like Larry. I had filed that winter night into the recesses of my consciousness. To me, it just never happened, and Larry was fast becoming a good friend. So, even though my parents objected, I continued to see him behind their backs. Whenever I could sneak away, whenever I could make an excuse, I did. Was I ever stupid!

Looking back, I wish my parents had locked me in my room and not let me out of their sight. I wish they had sent me away to live somewhere exotic with some really cool relative to watch over me and make sure I stayed out of trouble. I wish they had done something—anything. It's not entirely fair to say that, though. What could they have done? I was a rebellious thirteen-year-old, and a resourceful one at that. Whatever they had done, I probably would have found a way to see him.

One night, Larry came by in his Chevy Impala convertible. I was waiting outside in the dark, and, as he drove up, he whispered, "Come on. I want to take you for a ride." I jumped in the car and we were off. Off to where, I didn't know, but it felt good—doing something I wasn't supposed to be doing with someone I wasn't supposed to be with.

It was another chilly night, not as chilly as THAT night, but plenty cool nonetheless. Larry had the heat on full blast so that, even with the top down, the car was actually quite snug. The radio was cranked up, playing good ole country music, and he was swigging beer as he drove. Once we were away from my house, he steered the car onto the main road leading out of town. He was laughing, smiling, cracking jokes, and I was enjoying myself, listening to him, smelling his cologne, feeling the warm air come out of the vent, looking at the stars.

About twenty minutes later, he pulled onto an old dirt road. I had no idea where we were, so nonchalantly asked him, "Where are we going, Larry?"

He just shook his head. "Nowhere special."

So I shrugged and kept looking out the window at the rather bleak view. Nothing but dust as far as the eye could see. But it was okay. I felt good. I felt safe.

Larry continued to drive farther and farther away from town, until, suddenly, he began to slow the vehicle, pulling it onto a square patch of dirt on the side of the road. The car came to a halt, he put the gear in park, took a good long swig of beer, and turned to me.

"Let's get out," he said.

That was fine with me. Maybe we'd sit on the hood, talk, look at the sky, feel the cool breeze. In my mind, it was going to be a nice night, so I did what he told me. I got out of the car, and, as the door closed behind me, I leaned against it, my arms crossed over my chest. Larry came around from the other side of the car, still with a beer in his hand. When he reached me, he downed the remnants of the alcohol and tossed the can onto the ground. Then, putting his arm around me, he led me to the rear of the car. Okay, so maybe we were going to sit on the trunk instead of the hood. Still, it would be nice.

A Nice Night

As we reached the back of the car, something changed in him. "Get down!" Larry commanded in a voice that was at once imperious and filled with deadly overtones.

A "What?" was all I could muster.

But, no sooner had I spoken, then he put his hands on my shoulders and kicked my legs out from under me, holding me as he shoved me onto the ground. The dirt was cold and hard, and, as he started undressing me, all I could think was, "Not again. Not again."

But there it was. Again. The same thing. I resisted more

than I had the first time, kicking him, beating him with my fists, even trying to pull his hair, but all to no avail. He was bigger, stronger, and soon was ripping off my clothes.

I kept fighting. As soon as he got my shirt off and started for my pants, I found my shirt and tried to put it back on. So he pulled it away and threw it on the ground. I tried to roll out from under him, but he grabbed me with one arm and pulled me back toward him. As he continued to try to force my pants down, I kept throwing my hands in between, making it harder for him to do what he wanted to do.

And then, suddenly, he went berserk, completely berserk. Standing up over me, he began kicking a Styrofoam chest, over and over again, while screaming, "Damn it, Trudy! What the hell did you come here for if you didn't want to do this?"

He threw his fists outward, then raised one hand and brought it down on the trunk of the car. "Fucking great. Just fucking great!" Turning back to me, he raised his hands to his head and started pulling at his hair. "Fucking shit! Fucking shit! Goddamn you!" Stomping around, kicking things, punching whatever he could find. I really thought he was going nuts.

And stupid me. Stupid little old me. Lying on the ground, doing nothing. Paralyzed again by fear. I think in the end it was the violence that got me, the sheer terror that he would kill me out here in the middle of nowhere. So, when he finally finished his tirade, he came back to me. And, this time, I did not resist too much. A few minutes and it was over. Just like before.

He rolled off me, stood, leaned against the car door, grabbed a beer, drank one after another, as I gathered my clothes and got back into the car where it was warm. I could hear him outside making noises, talking to himself, as I quickly dressed, then sat with my legs up against my chest.

I couldn't believe what had happened. Once again, I kept telling myself it had not, that this was a nightmare and I was going to wake up in a few minutes, look around, and see my animals snuggled up next to me. But I knew this was real, and I was blaming myself. It was all my fault. If I hadn't made him mad, if I hadn't argued, if I hadn't struggled, if I . . . .

A couple of hours passed before Larry slipped back into the driver's seat. Without saying a single word, he turned the ignition and started toward home. And, though the music was blaring, it was the most silent ride I had ever experienced.

When he pulled up to the front of my house, he said, slurring his words, "I'll talk to you in a few days." All I could do was look at him. Didn't he know what he had done? Didn't he care? I shook my head as he continued to drink, and, without looking back, I walked into the house. Somehow, I thought that if I didn't run, didn't panic, it would be all right. That not screaming and crying would somehow improve what had happened. I reached the door, and, finally, turned back, but Larry had already started away. Gone for now, but—unfortunately—not gone for good.

That night, I rocked myself to sleep yet again. This time, again, no tears would come.

Accident

The next day, a friend of mine called and told me Larry had been in a terrible wreck. Apparently something had upset him, and he'd missed a turn (on the same road we'd been on earlier), rolled the car, and was in the hospital with a head injury. She asked if I wanted to go see him with her and a few other friends. I really did not want to, not after it had happened again. I was done. It was over.

But, somehow, I felt guilty. I felt it was my fault he had tried to kill himself. Not that he was just stupid and had been drinking and had an accident. No, somehow I was to blame. So I went.

He looked terrible. Bruised and with bandages on his head and arms, he had trouble speaking and moving. He looked so bad, I felt sorry for him, and, when he hugged me and apologized for what had happened, I actually believed him. When he told me he couldn't live without me, I believed that, too.

And so, after he spent a few days in the hospital, I was back to my old game, sneaking around behind my parents' backs, fortunately without any further "incidents" like the two that had already happened.

Christmas came and went, and, with the new year, came prayers from my family for something better, something happier. Unfortunately, that was not to be. Right after the first of the year, my mother started questioning me about my period.

She and my father knew I was still dating Larry. They had stopped saying anything, but, every time they looked at me, I could tell they were disappointed. Then, one day, out of nowhere,

I came home and my mother followed as I slinked up to my room, opening the door I had just closed behind me.

I continued doing what I was doing, cleaning my room, putting things in their places, and, the whole time, I could feel my mother standing there, her eyes boring into me. Finally, she coughed slightly—her signal that it was time for me to pay her some respect. I turned and there she was, determined, her eyes steely, her hands on her hips.

"What?" I asked indignantly.

She looked away for a second as if she were embarrassed to ask the question, but, when her gaze returned to me, she let it out. One breath, one sentence—one fateful question. "Have you had your period this month?"

I stood there for several seconds, not sure how to answer. Or even what it had to do with anything. I knew what a period was, but I sure as heck did not know how it related to pregnancy. No one had ever told me *that*. I remember feeling nervous anyway, afraid that, no matter what I said, I might unleash the beast and receive another tirade on dating Larry. But, finally, I found the courage to answer.

"No," I responded, then went back to putting my stuffed animals in place. Nervously, frantically, I picked up one I had just put down and then replaced it, doing anything so I wouldn't have to face my mother. I could feel her still standing there; I knew she was still looking at me.

A minute passed, then two, and, finally, I heard her turn, walk out, and close the door behind her.

I don't know what happened next, whether she went right to my father, or whether she went off alone first to cry, or to plan some way to break off my relationship with Larry.

Whatever she did after the door closed, I fell to my bed and started to cry. What was I doing? What on earth was I doing? Then, as the tears faded, I found my resolve. Larry told me he loved me, and, despite everything that happened, I loved him, too. When he was treating me well, he was indeed treating me well, humoring me, kissing me, making me feel special. When he was treating me badly? I just put that out of my mind, forgetting it ever happened, each and every time.

The Birds and the Bees

So life continued. Another month went by. Another month when Larry and I were dating and, yes, having sex. Although our encounters were never truly voluntary on my part, I had stopped resisting; I just figured it was part of the relationship, part of love.

And, in the meantime, I avoided my mother. What was all this talk about my period anyway? Heck if I knew. What I did know was that it was pissing off my mother, and I went so far as to ask my sister if there was a way I could "fake it." Funny, heh? A little naïve? Certainly, but that is who I was. The birds and the bees? What was that?

Then the proverbial shit hit the fan. Early one weekend morning, cool but sunny—a nice day by all usual measurements—I had just gotten up and was getting ready to go downstairs for breakfast. That's when the door opened slowly. My mother stood there, a serious expression on her face. Even before I could protest that she had invaded my privacy, she motioned and said, "Come with me."

I followed her down the hall and into her bedroom. "Sit," she commanded as we reached the big queen-size bed. It was then I knew this was serious. Her bedroom, sitting on her bed, was the sign, the sign that what we were going to talk about was probably deep and unpleasant, fraught with possible consequences. I was afraid.

She sat down next to me as I folded my hands tightly in my lap, trying to prevent them from shaking. I had no idea what this was all about, but guessed it had to do with Larry. What else could it be? Turning, she looked me up and down for several seconds, then right in the eyes.

"Have you had your period this month?" she asked in a soft tone. I should have recognized that sign, too. That tone meant she was past anger, past disappointment, and in the realm of utter and complete devastation.

I shook my head. "No," I replied, not understanding why she kept asking me this question. What did it have to do with anything?

That's when the utter devastation became clear. Her face turned a dark shade of red, and her eyes began to tear. A few drops even made their way down her right cheek before she wiped them away. Breathing in deeply, apparently to control herself, she continued. "I want to ask you something." She paused, breathing in again, then said, "And I want you to know I already spoke with Larry." That was when her voice cracked, as if she were reaching a point of no return, her breaking point. What had I done?

"Have you had intercourse with Larry?"

I heard the words, but I had no idea what to say. What did she mean? "Intercourse?" I said out loud. "What is that?"

My mother was now having a hard time composing herself. I could see it in her eyes, in the way she shifted her body every few seconds, in the way she looked at me, at once full of disappointment, skepticism, and a glimmer—a slight glimmer—of hope. Then she dropped the bombshell. "Larry already said you did."

And still I did not know what she meant. What was intercourse? I looked at her, and, with all honesty, I answered, "Okay, I guess. If Larry said so, then . . . ."

That was what broke my mother. "Okay," she said in a tightly controlled tone as she stood up from the bed. "We're going to see a doctor tomorrow."

I nodded, said okay, and left.

You see I had never been told about "the birds and the bees." Not by my parents and certainly not in school. Intercourse, sex, period, pregnancy—these words I knew existed, but I did not know what they meant. Babies, and where they came from? I suppose I still thought that storks brought them. That may sound laughable, but, when nobody sits you down and tells you how you get pregnant and what it is to have a child, you just don't know. You're simply uninformed.

Doctor's Appointment

The next day, my mother woke me up early. We went the two miles down the road into town and checked in at the clinic. "Trudy has a ten o'clock appointment with Dr. Martin." The woman looked at her sheet, nodded, then pointed to a few chairs in the small waiting room.

We sat in silence for several minutes as I grew increasingly nervous. "OB/GYN" read the sign on the door. What kind of doctor was that? I looked around. Two other girls were also waiting, both bulging in the stomach. I KNEW they were pregnant, but what was I doing here?

Then a woman came out and called my mother's name.

My mother turned to me. "Wait here," she said, and then followed the woman into the back. I sat there alone for several more minutes, now wondering just what my mother and the doctor were talking about. Wondering what this whole visit was about. Wondering what it had to do with Larry. Wondering what it had to do with my period and with "intercourse."

I would soon find out.

Five minutes later, the same nurse came out and called me to come back. She led me to the bathroom, gave me a small plastic cup, and told me to urinate in it. I did, and, when I came out, she took the cup from me. Then she drew some blood from my arm. In an exam room, she had me sit on a table.

The doctor came in, and, without speaking, started to examine me. "Uh huh," he said as he looked at my "privates." "Uh huh," he repeated. It took only a few minutes, and, when he was done, he smiled and asked me to have a seat in the waiting room.

I waited two minutes... five... ten, growing increasingly nervous. Somehow, I sensed there was something terribly serious going on, but nobody had told me anything.

When my mother walked out, I KNEW something terrible had happened. Her eyes were swollen and red, her cheeks tearstained. She didn't even look at me, simply commanded, "Let's go," as she walked by. On the ride home, my mother was completely silent. And I was too afraid to speak.

The News

A day passed, and nothing came of the doctor's visit. Not a word from my mother or my father, and my nervousness began to fade. Maybe it was nothing after all. Another day passed, and my fears abated even more, to the point where I'd almost forgotten the whole thing had even happened.

But, the next evening, I was watching the orange ball of fire that was the setting sun through the window in my room, busy doing something, when I heard low whispers—my parents trying to be quiet. Then, their voices got louder... and louder... and louder.

So I did what I always did when my parents yelled. I pretended I couldn't hear it, and played teacher with my pets. It was time for their math lesson. For an hour, I drowned out the noise with my play, but, even so, I could feel the tension building.

I was just about to give my pets their math homework for the night when the door opened, only a few inches, but enough for my mother to poke her head in. "Trudy, come downstairs," she said. It was not a question or a wish. It was quite simply a demand.

She left immediately, and I knew there was no disobeying. Not this time. So I followed. When I passed the living room, I saw my father staring at me. His blue eyes were cold and angry and full of disappointment. Terrible, terrible disappointment. And it was then I finally realized something really was wrong.

My mother motioned for me to sit at the kitchen table. She sat across from me and I could see the venom in her expression. Her lips pursed, her eyes steely, she was angry, disappointed, ready to explode. But she remained controlled and cold.

"You've been one naughty girl." A statement. One I did not understand but which shook me to the core anyway. "What are you doing having sex at your age?" she asked accusingly, again the venom very much at the surface.

The truth is, at this point, I knew what sex was, although I still had no idea how one became pregnant. For all I knew, all you had to do was kiss. But I could not answer my mother. Not directly at least, so I just shrugged my shoulders.

That did not sit well with her. Whatever anger she'd been holding in now boiled to the surface. "Well?" she screamed. "Good going, Trudy! Now you're pregnant!"

When I heard those words, I sat in stunned silence. Pregnant? Pregnant? How could I be pregnant?

I looked at my mother, and I could see that she was telling me the truth. And I became paralyzed. I was having a baby? How? Why? What? I was in shock.

"That's right," my mother said. "You're pregnant." She stood up, pushing her chair back forcefully, When she reached the kitchen door, she turned back to me. "You have another appointment with the doctor in a few days. Until then, I don't want you to discuss anything. Not here in this house. Not outside. Not with your friends. Not with me. And certainly not with your father. Do you understand?"

I nodded submissively, and, as she left, I felt as if I'd been dropped in the middle of the ocean and told to swim to shore all by myself. That night, afraid, I cried myself to sleep.

Chapter 5

Thirteen and Pregnant

I didn't speak to my parents for the next three days. To say it was uncomfortable was an understatement. My father avoided me as much as possible. When I came down to eat, he would get up and leave the rest of us to eat in complete silence. The tension was so great, the silence so profound, even the clang of a fork or knife against a plate sent shivers down my spine.

When it was time to go back to the doctor, my mother made sure I was dressed appropriately and then drove me the two miles into town. Again in silence. We waited a few minutes, again without sharing a word, then the nurse called us back. She led us to his nice, comfortable office, his diplomas and certifications displayed on the wall behind his desk. We sat in two chairs in front of him as he opened what must have been my file.

Evidently my mother had let him know I was aware of the pregnancy, for, when he began to speak, he did so directly to me. "Well," he said, "you have a few options. First, you can have the baby and give it up for adoption." My mother shook her head from side to side as the doctor continued. "You can also fly out to California and have an abortion. It's still legal there." Again my mother shook her head, this time more vigorously. "She's NOT having an abortion."

Meanwhile, I was beginning to panic. Adoption? Abortion? What did all this mean? Abortion? I had never heard the word. What was going on? How could I be pregnant?

As the doctor spoke, I kept looking at my stomach. It wasn't bulging. I didn't feel anything. I could not believe there was a baby growing in there. I did not want to believe there was a baby growing in there. My God! How did this happen? How could this be?

The doctor glanced at my mother after she had made her pronouncement, nodded, then turned back to me. "Well then, the only other choice is for her to keep the baby and raise it herself."

The doctor continued to speak but I did not hear a word. I had become completely disassociated from the reality I was facing.

My mind was swimming. Baby. Child. Crying. Hungry. I was thirteen-years-old. How the hell was I going to raise a child? I wanted to ask. What about adoption? What about an abortion? But I couldn't. My mother had made it very clear I had only one option. Raising it myself. Then I heard the doctor's voice again. "Well, you don't have to make a decision now, but in the next few weeks." He smiled, my mother thanked him, and he ushered us out.

When we arrived at home, my mother finally spoke, telling me to go to my room and stay there until I was called. My father had not said a word to me in three weeks and he didn't start now. Later that night, my mother called me down and sat me on the couch across from her and my father. I had never seen my father like that before. He was cold and angry, and he looked at me only briefly. When he did, I could see in his eyes the utter disappointment.

"Larry said he would marry you," my mother began. "Now, do you want to marry him?"

I never got the chance to answer. My father spoke up for the first time. "She's gonna marry him!" he announced, then shot up and stormed out. There was never any more discussion. That was it. That was my fate. I was to marry Larry.

Isolation

That night, I went into the bathroom, my mind racing. I was going to have to marry Larry? What would that mean? How would I live? And I was going to have his baby?

I sat on the toilet, put my head in my hands, and started to cry. How could I get out of this?

And then I looked down at the bathtub. It was deep enough, to be sure. I could do it. I could really do it. It would be so easy. Fill the tub with water, take my clothes off, submerge myself until I couldn't breathe. I wanted to do it. I wanted to do it so badly. To end this charade. This awful, awful thing. To escape from this reality. It seemed so easy. So promising.

Then it hit me. If I did that, my father would see me naked. And I knew right then, I couldn't pull it off. I cried some more, and wished that, somehow, some way, God would take me and release me from this burden.

So there I was, pregnant with a child who would be only slightly more needy than myself. I went to school for a few more weeks, then my parents forced me to drop out. Nobody knew I was pregnant yet. They just thought I'd gained a few pounds.

My parents were not eager to tell anyone, including the family. I felt completely isolated, totally alone, and it didn't help matters when word began finally to spread that I was indeed pregnant.

Still nobody ever talked about it. Nobody. Not my parents, not my grandparents, not any other member of my family. The fact was just there, like some looming dark cloud.

At best, I felt embarrassed—embarrassed I was fat, embarrassed I'd been so naïve, embarrassed I'd gotten pregnant, but, most of all, embarrassed by the way people looked at me. It was 1970, and teenaged pregnancy in South Texas was no more common than water in the desert. We were all God-fearing Christians. Pregnant at thirteen? Unheard of. So, I soon lost all my friends as well. Their parents would not allow them to hang out with me.

I had nobody.

I spent most of the next few weeks in my room. My father was still not saying a word to me. He and my mother and sister and I would eat dinner in complete silence. Every once in a while, my sister would try to start a conversation. "So I got a B on my test," she said once. My mother only glared at her, and that was the end of that.

My sister, in fact, was carrying around a burden of guilt I didn't know about. Only later in life did I learn that my mother had approached her after it had come to light that I was having sex, and admonished her, "Why weren't you watching your sister?"

But how could she have been? She was only sixteen at the time, a child herself. It was not her responsibility to be watching me. I don't blame her one bit. Not at all. I made the choice. I am the only one to blame.

Too Young

So, a few weeks later, Larry and I and my parents made our way to the county clerk's office. I was in a nice dress, Larry in

47

what passed for a suit. When we arrived, my father told the county clerk he wanted Larry and me to marry. The clerk asked how old I was. "Thirteen," he said. The clerk shook his head. "Even with parental consent, she's too young."

My father stood there for a few seconds, unsuccessfully controlling his rage, then turned and walked back to the car. He dropped Larry off, then drove us back to our house, where I was summarily sent to my room.

I could hear my parents talking that night. I could hear my father raising his voice. I could feel the tension, the anger.

I thought about the bathtub again. How warm the water would be. How easy it would be just to drift off. But I couldn't do it. And so, for the hundredth time in the last few months, I cried myself to sleep.

It soon became apparent that my parents had decided that Larry and I would be married, come hell or high water. One day, my mother woke me up early and told me to put on the dress I had worn for a ballroom dance class when I was twelve. I also put on white frosted lipstick, but, when she saw me, she said, "Wipe that off, Trudy, and put some of this on," handing me her dark red lipstick. "At the very least, you're going to need to look older."

We got in the car, picked up Larry, and crossed over into Mexico near Laredo. My father had heard that you could get married in Mexico, and it would be recognized in the United States.

When we arrived in a small town, my father had us wait in the car as he went inside to talk to a judge. Larry tried to make conversation, but my mother was in no mood. She gave him a look, and that was the end of that. We waited five minutes, ten minutes. I would have given anything to get out of that car and run. Just run. Anywhere. But, instead, I sat there twiddling my thumbs and trying to tell myself everything would be okay.

A few minutes later, my father came out, his head hanging down. As he got in the car, he turned the ignition and started toward home. My mother did not even have to ask the question. "She's too young," he said, and that was the end of the conversation and of trying to get married in Mexico.

Wedding Day

A few days later, my father came home with an old

typewriter he had borrowed from work, one of those black, heavy, mechanical ones, with the large keys. He and my mother talked in the kitchen, where he had set the typewriter down on the table. I stood in the living room, watching and listening surreptitiously.

"She's gotta be fifteen to get married," he said to my mother, "and damned if she's not going to get that done." My mother handed him a piece of paper with a red embossed seal toward the bottom. Later, I found out it was my birth certificate. My father loaded the paper into the typewriter, positioned it carefully. He pressed one button, then another. He studied his handiwork, then gently pulled the paper out of the typewriter. "She's fifteen now," he said dryly. My mother stood silent as I secretly watched, my heart aching.

The next day was my wedding day. I had always dreamed I would have a grand ceremony with all my friends and family in attendance, everybody smiling and happy. In my dream, my beaming father walked me down the aisle while everyone said, "Doesn't she look beautiful?" When we reached the altar, my father would lean in, kiss me, then squeeze my hand tightly as he slowly stepped back.

I would turn and there would be the love of my life. Although I never could see his face, I knew he was kind and gentle and loving, and he treated me with respect.

But that was just a dream.

The reality was more utilitarian. My mother had me wear my red floral dress with pouffy shoulders. She did my makeup—lipstick and rouge, to make me look older. There was nothing romantic about any of it. My mother barely said a word to me, and, when Larry arrived, my father insisted we all get in the car immediately and "get this thing over with."

Soon, we arrived in Goliad, a small town about a half hour from home, where nobody knew us. My father had called ahead, so the justice of the peace was waiting in his chambers when we entered the town hall. The judge took the altered birth certificate, and, within minutes, Larry and I were married.

No father walked me down the aisle. Nobody said how pretty I looked. And there was no husband who treated me with kindness and respect. Just Larry and I in front of a justice of the peace while my parents tried to pretend they were happy.

By this time, I really didn't care—about anything. I was just going through the motions, doing whatever I was told to do, no longer offering any resistance.

In retrospect, I cannot see how my father could have turned me over to such a monster. Not that he knew Larry had raped me. But, still, it hurt all the same. I feared Larry. I feared him more than I feared God. I always felt I was walking on pins and needles when I was around him, that at any moment he could go into one of his tirades.

But there we were, standing before the justice of the peace. "I now pronounce you man and wife," the judge said. Larry leaned down and kissed me once, a little peck on the lips, and it was over. I was thirteen, pregnant, and married to a dangerously abusive drunk.

I knew I was sliding down a slippery slope. I could sense myself falling, falling, falling, into a bottomless pit, with nothing to grab onto, and nothing to hold me up.

I knew it was bad. But I did not know how truly bad it was going to get.

The Stairs

For awhile, we lived with my parents, in an upstairs room. Larry couldn't afford an apartment, let alone a house. I lay there every night next to him, more than a little afraid, my stomach getting bigger and bigger. Larry would fall asleep, but I remained awake with my thoughts. "Just go away!" I would tell the bulge in my midsection. "Why can't you just go away?" And then I would turn over, curl up as tightly as I could, and cry myself to sleep, hoping I would wake up to find it was all just a terrible nightmare.

But, inevitably, morning would come and I would have to face the truth again. Larry would go off to work about the same time as my father, and I'd sit on the couch in the living room and watch television.

I remember once watching a movie in which a pregnant woman fell down the stairs, losing her baby in the process. I thought, "I could do that, and it would all be over. I'd be free of Larry, and could go back to being a kid again, to playing with my animals and my friends at school." I wasn't truly conscious of the fact that there was a precious baby growing inside me.

So I walked to the steps. Wood creaked as I started up. I got about halfway, then turned and looked behind me. Wow! It was a long way down.

I was tired and it was warm. I began to perspire as I continued to make my way up to the landing. Three steps to go, two. One. I reached the top, slowly turned, looked down. My stomach hung out about a foot over the first tread. As I stood there, ready to take the plunge, I prayed, "God, please help me!"

Silently crying, I slowly slid onto the end of the top step, still holding the railing. I said another prayer—all the while wanting to scream out—then closed my eyes and let go.

I tumbled down the stairs, one after the other, praying the entire time: "Lord, please get me out of this situation. Please, do what you must!" Pain shot through my shoulder as I hit one step very hard. I finally cried out, even as I tumbled some more. Then, suddenly, I was at the bottom, lying on the floor on my side.

My mother came running. "Oh, my God! Are you okay?" I winced at the pain in my shoulder, and my mother helped me up. "You've got to be careful," she said naïvely. She drove me directly to the doctor, who examined me, assured my mother everything was all right, and said, "She should stay in bed for a few days."

And so I did. Regretting that I couldn't even fall down the stairs right.

Choices

As I write this, I feel a tremendous amount of guilt for having wanted to lose my baby. My son has turned out to be a wonderful, caring, compassionate man. He is creative and loving, fun and dynamic, despite being born of a barely fourteen-year-old mother and an abusive alcoholic father. I cannot imagine not having him in my life.

So, in retrospect, I am glad I did not succeed in ending my pregnancy that day. And I'm glad my mother refused me the chance at an abortion. Not that I condemn those who do go that route. If I'd even known I had that choice, I might have taken that way out, but, as fate would have it, I didn't, and so I am blessed with a kind and caring son who is an asset to the world and to my life. I wouldn't have it any other way.

At the time, though, I could not think any positive thoughts. I could not laugh. I could not even smile. I no longer seemed a participant in my own life, a surreal existence in which I watched helplessly from afar as I spiraled out of control into an abyss.

Larry and I were married in January 1970. Within a few months, I was huge. So huge I could barely get around. I waddled from place to place like some penguin on the Antarctic ice shelf. Now, it seems kind of funny. But, at the time, I was certainly depressed. Why not? By late summer, I was a pregnant fourteen-year-old who had gained almost half her own weight. But, even though I had thought about suicide, I had never acted on it. Instead, I just kept on keeping on, like a good girl—like a good, Texas-loving, God-fearing, Christian girl.

August 29 was an extremely hot day, even for South Texas. By this time, Larry and I were living in a house across the street from the beauty shop in which my mother worked. We'd pulled the mattress from our bed into the living room because it was the only room in which there was an air conditioner. But I was still hot, and I was tired.

The doctor had told me I should not have sex; it was too dangerous and the baby could get an infection. But Larry kept insisting. He said he loved me. Ha! What he loved was a case of beer and a few minutes' romp in bed. Even at fourteen I knew that.

That hot night, Larry forced himself on me as he always did. I was never a truly willing participant in any sexual encounter with him—ever, although one can argue that, when I did not put up a fight, at the very least I acquiesced. The fact remains, though, that my will had been suborned. I was beaten into constant submission. He'd get on top of me as I lay there; he'd do his thing, then roll over, and, for a few moments, I felt free, as if he could never hurt me again. But, a few nights later, the same thing would happen again. Occasionally, I resisted, but then he'd go into a tirade, and, well, he was stronger than I was, physically and mentally.

Now it seems strange, but I simply didn't know I had any other options. Not a clue.

Of course, there were not as many sources of help available then as there are now, but I felt I there were none at all. And to all the women who still think like that, who feel helpless and hopeless: you DO have options. You really do. You just have to make the choice to seek out those who can, and will, help you.

Maybe I wouldn't have done anything differently. Maybe I would have stayed with Larry. Who knows? But least it would have been my decision, my choice. I prayed to know what to do on many occasions, then and later. But I saw no way out. Not yet.

The next morning, August 30, I woke up with terrible back pain. It felt like my muscles were in constant spasm. Larry had already gone to work, so I called my mother. "It sounds like you're in labor," she said. "I'll be over in a minute."

It barely took her that long. When I answered the door, bent over at my waist from the pain, she looked me up and down, then said, "We've got to do something about your hair."

In retrospect, that sounds crazy! Childbirth is dangerous. Women die. And my mother was concerned about my hair?

But I was a kid, so I did as I was told. She sat me down on the couch and tenderly put my hair up in a yellow ribbon, even as I was doubled over in pain. That day, I have to give my mother credit. She was full of kindness, tenderness, and support. Her voice had a soothing quality, and her strokes were loving. I remember thinking, "I wish it was always like this."

Childbirth

My hair done, she drove me to the hospital, and I was quickly put into a room where I continued in labor. As usual, I was clueless. Nobody had told me a thing about what was going to happen, what to expect, what they would do to me. Nada. Nothing.

The doctor had told my mother, of course, and he assumed she had told me. And my mother assumed the doctor had discussed it directly with me. But no one had. And the pain. Oh, the pain! It was excruciating, beyond anything I had ever experienced.

A nurse came over with a small tub and razor. "We're going to give you an enema and shave you, okay?" she said as she prepared her tools. And then, without warning, I freaked. I mean, I totally freaked.

I started yelling and screaming, "No!!!!! No!!!! Get me the hell out of here!!!! No!!!!" The nurse looked at me as if I were possessed by the devil himself, and called a colleague. Together, they tried to hold me down as I thrashed about on the bed. "Get me out of here! No!!!"

Finally the nurse put restraints on my arms and legs and tied them to the bed railing so tightly I couldn't move. Which made me freak out even more. They gave me a "shot" to "calm me down," and, after about twenty minutes, the medicine started to take effect. I settled down, too tired and too drugged to do or say anything except wince when the contractions came.

Five hours later, they took me into the delivery room where my arms and legs were strapped down, and my feet put in stirrups. I was in so much pain, it seemed unbearable. And, as usual, I was all alone.

In the delivery room, the doctor cajoled me. "Push, Trudy, push. Come on Trudy . . . breathe, breathe, breathe." The pain was so great, I wanted to die, literally, there and then. "No more!" I kept saying to myself as the tears rolled down my face. "Please God, no more!"

I pushed one more time, and, suddenly, felt this incredible release as something passed between my legs. And then I heard the noise. The noise of a baby's first cries. MY baby's first cries. As they cut the cord and cleaned him off, I slumped back in my bed, exhausted and beaten.

I don't know how long I was out from the drugs, maybe only an hour or so, but, when I woke up, my mother and father were standing over my bed. "You look so sad," my mother said as she stroked my hair. "A frail little girl with a yellow ribbon," she added, smiling.

I looked up at her and at my father, not expecting anything. Not really. Maybe I was sad, but I know now it must have broken their hearts to see me, their own fourteen-year-old daughter, having just gone through childbirth. They stayed until a nurse came in and said I needed to get some rest. So, my parents left, and I was in the room alone—very, very alone.

I saw the baby a few times over the next forty-eight hours, whenever they brought him to me to feed. The nurse showed me what to do, how to position the baby, how to hold his head. It all felt surreal, and, to be quite honest, I really didn't care. I was too afraid of the responsibility and of not knowing what to do. I was completely overwhelmed.

A Family

I don't know where Larry was throughout all this, but, a couple of days later, he came to pick up me and James—our baby. Just before he arrived, the nurse told me she was going to bring James in so I could change and dress him. I froze. What was I going to do? I picked up the phone, and, in a state of panic, called my mother. "What's wrong, Trudy?" she asked.

"Mom, oh Mom, they are bringing the baby in for me to change. How am I going to change a diaper?" I cried. "I don't know how to hold him, or clean him, or dress him!" I started pulling at my hair. "Mom, what am I going to do?"

Whether she heard the fear in my voice, I do not know, and I guess it doesn't matter. "It'll come naturally, Trudy," she said quietly. "Just do what comes naturally." All I could think was, "What the hell does that mean? What kind of advice is that?"

When they brought me the baby, my thoughts raced. Thoughts of fear, of desperation. Why doesn't someone come and rescue me? Take the baby and care for him? How can my parents think that I can be responsible for a tiny, fragile, human being?

What about the nurses? Why don't they do more? Say something encouraging? Give me a sense that I can do this? Maybe they did. Maybe I just didn't hear it. Or maybe they'd been told to mind their own business.

"Where are all the adults in my life!" I wanted to scream, so loudly that the whole world would hear me. I was fourteen! "Hello! Hello! Can't you see I am a kid? What am I supposed to do here? Is anyone there? Can anyone hear me? Help me, please, please, someone help me."

The tears began to flow and flow and flow, running down onto my already drenched gown. "How can I, Trudy, take care of this precious baby?" But no one was there to listen. No one was there to hear me. I was truly alone.

Now I am not a fool. I now have many years of experience behind me and have had time to reflect—and I still can't get over the fact that a fourteen-year-old is ever given the responsibility to take care of a child. Maybe, just maybe, there are some who are mature enough to handle it. But there cannot be many. And I was certainly not one of them.

Look around you. Look at the thirteen- and fourteen-year-olds you know, from school or church, your own children or children of friends or coworkers, girls you see at the mall or studying at the library. Would you ever think of handing them a three-day-old infant to care for? Would you say, "Here you go. Take care of this baby, and the best advice I have is it will come naturally"? Would you then leave them be? I don't think so. But that was the situation I was in.

And so it was just me and the baby, and, of course,

Larry—drunken, crazy, abusive Larry. But that was the life that had come my way. My fate.

We went home that night, the three of us—a family.

Chapter 6

Sugar and Spice and Everything Not So Nice

Our first night together as a family. In my dreams, I was still imagining that special wedding day and night. As a younger child, I had imagined my husband would carry me over the threshold as I snuggled in his arms, laughing quietly, partly out of fatigue and partly from the champagne I held in my hand.

He would take me to the bed, drop me gently onto my back, then lie beside me, gently stroking my hair, as I gazed into his eyes and wondered how I came to be so lucky to be married to this wonderful man.

Instead, I was with Larry. No threshold. No champagne. No gentleness. With Larry, everything was rough. His mannerisms, his speech, his actions. Everything.

I don't recall our first night as a family very well, if at all, having blocked out most of it. And for good reason. I was barely into my teens, with a child to take care of, and married to an alcoholic and abusive man.

In retrospect, I realize I could have curled up into the fetal position and surrendered. In some ways, I did, later on. But, in other ways, I fought the good fight. Tried to make things work. Tried to find some common ground.

We never did find any, but that is not the point. Life is often about struggle. You find yourself in a position you don't like, and struggle to get out of it. It took me awhile, but I finally succeeded. That doesn't make what I went through any easier, but does make it worthwhile in the end. At least, that is how I look at it now.

What I do remember about that night is being scared, so scared I cannot accurately put it into words. The best I can do is remind you of that feeling you had when you were young and your parents left you alone for the very first time. You sat there wondering what to do with yourself . . . wondering if they would ever come back . . . wondering if you would be alone for the rest of your life.

That feeling was what overcame me that night. I was all alone. With Larry, sure. But, still, all alone because I had to face my "husband" every day. I was the one who had to put up with his drinking. I had to face being sexually assaulted, night after night, and being beaten when he felt like raging.

As I said, I was all alone.

Except now I had a child to take care of, a newborn baby boy, needy and desperate.

Just like me.

Motherhood

But my baby did have someone to depend on—me—his only source of food. Breastfeeding? What the hell did I know about that? People say it's easy. You just put the baby to your nipple and it starts suckling. But there's a lot more to it than that, like positioning, hygiene, burping, and, of course, there's the initial general discomfort. That's a lot for any woman to handle, let alone a fourteen-year-old who hasn't been taught much of anything about life other than the very basics.

But I persevered. I figured things out the best I could. I remember the first time I changed James's diaper. A stinker! I almost panicked as I saw the mess he had made. Covering my nose, I cleaned him up, put the soiled diaper in the laundry and a clean one on James. And, when I was finished, I gave myself a little pat on the back. It was an important moment for me, a moment in which I realized I could indeed take care of him, hold him, nurture him, feed him, take care of all his needs, at least for a little while.

I felt good knowing this—worthwhile. And I needed that because, for sure, Larry wasn't helping me feel good about myself at all.

Family Life

Larry and I and now James were all living in the small, older house across the street from the beauty shop in which my mother worked. The front door opened directly into the living/dining room. To the right were swinging doors into a kitchen barely big enough for the three of us. A small table sat against the wall next to a door that led to the garage. Another door on another wall led outside to the yard.

On the wall in the house's hallway hung a yellow phone, right out of the 1970s—bright, obnoxious, rotary, old. But I thought it was the coolest thing I had ever seen. Why? Can't say for sure. Maybe because it was my lifeline to the outside world? When I was on the phone, things didn't seem so bad. And it was vivid and colorful, joyous and fun, in an otherwise dark place.

Larry and I only stayed together two years, but those two years were the worst of my life. Larry spent most of our money on booze and, probably, other women, although I have no proof of that. We were dirt poor, and, after buying basic necessities for the baby, there was little money even for groceries.

We lived on beans and bologna. The beans were heated in a pot, the bologna fried in a pan. Lunch and dinner, five or six days a week. Occasionally, we did eat something else. If I'd been lucky, I'd been able to buy some peanut butter. But, mostly, it was beans and fried bologna, fried bologna and beans.

I don't think Larry minded. As long as he had something to fill his empty stomach, he was fine. He'd work (sometimes), eat, go out drinking, come home, and eat again. I took care of James and did some cleaning. That was our life, day in and day out.

I had hoped things would improve after we got married. Then I had hoped Larry would see James and take some responsibility for himself, and for his wife and child. But I was fooling myself. Larry wasn't going to change—I see that now. But then? Then I thought, if I fought with him enough, he would listen to me, hear me, undergo a transformation into my dream husband. You know. The kind that goes to work, comes home, kisses me hello, and says, "Hi honey, how was your day?"

Ozzie and Harriet we were not. Heck, we weren't even the Ozzie Osbournes!

A "Good" Day

There was little love in that house, and not even much affection between Larry and me. Occasionally, he was nice, but, after awhile, the Jekyll and Hyde routine becomes tiresome. Meanwhile, I was Cinderella without the glass slipper and without any hope of being rescued by a fairy godmother.

"Do the damned dishes!" Larry would yell. "Why the fuck isn't this place clean? What the hell do you do all day while I'm at work? You stupid bitch!"

I would stand there, taking it, until he was through, then run upstairs and try to hide. But, more often than not, he would follow me, still yelling and screaming. Sometimes he hit me.

One night, James was in the bedroom sleeping and I was in the kitchen cooking up yet another pot of beans—the cheap store brand, if I recall correctly—the kind with so much sugar in it, you can't even taste the beans. I was standing over the stove, an apron around my waist, stirring the pot and daydreaming. (I did that often—my way of escaping the hell in which I found myself.)

Larry came home from work in a bad mood, worse even than usual. I may have smiled at him—a weak, innocent, hopeful smile—a smile nonetheless. Did that set him off? I don't recall, but something did and he suddenly went into a rage. "You fucking bitch!" he screamed. "You fucking making me beans again? Can't you cook any fucking thing else?"

By now, I was used to the abuse and had figured out that, if I just turned my head, sometimes he would simply blow off steam and then forget about me. I did exactly that now, turning my attention toward the stove and the beans as Larry continued to rave. Two minutes. Three minutes. Five minutes. Usually, after a couple of minutes of yelling at the top of his lungs, he would have had enough.

But this time, he kept going, kept screaming at me. Finally, as I continued to ignore him, I heard the thump, thump, thump of his boots as he approached me. "What the fuck do you think you're doing? Ignoring me?" he cried as he put his hand over mine on the pot handle. I didn't look up. Kept my eyes fixed on the pot. Larry continued, "Who the fuck do you think you are?"

Then I made a mistake. I looked up, and, when I did, he grabbed me around the waist with one hand and picked up the pot of beans with the other. "I'm not gonna eat this fucking crap!" he screamed as he threw the pot toward the wall. Beans were spilling everywhere, and I gasped as he pushed me toward the mess. "You crazy bitch!" he cried, shoving me onto my hands and knees where the beans had fallen to the floor. The bottom half of my body was now covered in the brown sauce.

Larry pushed my head down. "Fucking clean this place

up!" He gave my head one more solid thrust, almost breaking my neck, then flung open the door to the garage, got in his car, and drove off, leaving me on the floor, covered in beans, crying.

And that was a good day!

For at least he hadn't beaten me. At least he hadn't sexually assaulted me. So many other days and nights were filled with just such nightmarish abuse, days and nights I wanted to die . . . days and nights I wouldn't wish on anyone . . . days and nights I'd like to pretend never happened. But they did.

Visitors

Like the time a bunch of girls pulled up in front of the house and Larry went outside to talk to them. I watched him out there, drinking beer, flirting. And I was enraged. How the hell could he do this to me? To his son? Right in front of his home? Where everyone could see? Where I could see? As if it did not even matter to him that he was "cheating"?

I stood at the door watching for several minutes, until one of the girls touched his arm. That was it. "Larry? Who are you talking to?" I asked from the porch.

"None of your fucking business!" He didn't even turn around.

I stood there, wanting to say something, wanting to scream, to tell him what an asshole he was, to go to hell, that I was taking James and leaving him. But the truth of the matter was, I had nowhere to go. So, I did the next best thing. I showed my righteous indignation by standing there with my arms crossed, waiting for him to turn around and see that I was still there.

Several more minutes passed before that happened, during which he continued flirting with the girls, and they with him. For, despite his beer breath, his cursing, and his overall bad demeanor, girls liked him. Wanted him. Wanted to be with him. He had this charming, almost sick charisma, that drew women toward him.

Women like me. If only I had known! If only they knew!

Finally, he turned, saw me out of the corner of his eye, and did a double take as if he weren't expecting me to show any backbone. I could see the look in his eye when he saw me standing there. I could see the rage. Suddenly, he jerked his body downward, picked up some gravel, and threw it at the porch, hitting me in the arms and torso.

"Get back in the fucking house!" he yelled, as he pelted me again and again. One after another after another, the rocks bit, stung me, even as I held up my hands to protect my face. Finally, I ran into the house, up the stairs into the bedroom, slammed the door behind me, and, sinking my head into the pillow, allowed the tears to stream down my face.

Survival

Of course, there were also the obligatory beatings. One night, we had come back from a party and were sitting in the car in the driveway. Larry was wasted—drunker than I had ever seen him, and I had indeed seen him drunk. He was bad enough sober, but when he was wasted? A psychopath. Homicidal even.

After he put the car in park, he leaned in and kissed me a couple of times. But I'd had a long day and a long night, and I wanted nothing but to get inside and go to sleep. My mother had James for the night, so all I really wanted to do was sleep until morning, then stay in bed for a few more hours, recharging my batteries and getting ready to take care of James again.

But Larry wouldn't listen. Instead, as I pulled away from him, he began to throw a fit. His face red, he asked, "What, you don't want me? What's the fucking matter? You cheating on me?"

Words I thought I would never hear. Me? Cheating on him? When would I have had the time? When, in fact, would he let me out of the house? Never!

I tried to remain calm, tried to improve the situation by responding in as controlled a tone as I could. "No, Larry," I said. "Of course not."

Maybe it was my soft, tired voice. Maybe it was the night. Maybe it was me. Or maybe, just maybe, it was all Larry. Whatever it was, he flew off the handle, just like he had the night with the beans, only this time, he was even more violent.

"You fucking did it, didn't you, bitch?" he screamed.

I threw my hands up over my face in anticipation of the beating. I was so very tired, and I didn't want this. Not this night. Not ever again.

"No!" I cried, as the tears began streaming down my face. "N—"

Larry answered before I could finish. "You're fucking cheating!"

I denied it again. He yelled again. I denied it once more. He accused me another time. I told him he was crazy. Then, he threw his hand out, put it behind my head, and pushed my face up against the window, hard enough that my neck felt like it was going to snap.

"Tell me you did it!" he screamed, as he pushed harder, my cheekbone aching as it pressed against the glass. "Tell me you did it!"

"No!" I cried, sobbing, terrified. "No, Larry, I didn't!"

By this time, I was shaking uncontrollably. He pulled back his arm, then hit me across the face. "Tell me you did it!" he screamed yet again.

"No!" He hit me again. "No!" And again. "No!"

"Tell me you did it, and I'll leave you alone."

Leave me alone. Leave me alone. The words reverberated in my mind. Was he being honest? Would he . . . leave me alone? At that point, I had no more fight left in me. Here was a way out, a glimmer of hope. All I had to do was say three simple words. "Okay!" I screamed. "I did it."

There. There it was. I had said it. No matter that it wasn't true. It was my release. My refuge. At least, so I hoped.

For a few seconds, Larry remained still. Quiet. I thought indeed he might leave me be, might keep his promise. But this was Larry. After that calm in which you could have heard a needle falling to the ground, Larry began to shake to the point I thought he might be having a seizure. I even thought he might be dying. But I didn't care. Not after all the beatings. Not after all the emotional and mental abuse. His dying would be my way out.

I thought about running into the house and locking the door. Even if he had his key, he'd never have been able to put it in the lock, not as drunk as he was. Then I remembered with whom I was dealing. Larry probably would just have broken a window and climbed in, or, worse, driven the car right through the front of the house.

So I sat there, numb, waiting, anticipating what was to come. What did come was the worst beating I had ever taken. He grabbed my head and smacked it against the seat and window. He hit me with open palms and clenched fist. He hit me hard and he hit me often. All the while, I was screaming. "Stop! Larry! Pl-e-e-e-a-a-a-a-s-s-s-e-e-e-e! Stop!" I protected my head and face as best I could, but I couldn't stop him, couldn't fight back.

Then, suddenly, I felt as if everything slowed down, as if I were out of my body watching from above. I could see Larry hitting me. Could see him raging. But from above. I still have no idea how much time passed. But, as suddenly as it had begun, it was over.

I came back to my body to find Larry sitting there, silently. As if nothing had happened, he looked at me, said, "It's getting hot in here," opened the door, and walked into the house. Just like that.

Numbly, I looked around the car. Things were strewn all over—beer cans, pieces of paper, cigarettes, ashes. And there was blood. Not a lot, but enough. On the window and on the dashboard, was my blood, from a cut above my eye.

I could feel the blood flowing down my face, and I dabbed it with my finger. Warm. Wet. I looked at my hand, saw the dark red liquid, saw my fingers shaking uncontrollably, then grabbed one hand with the other to try to stop the tremors.

Was it over? Was it really over? Frantically, I looked toward the house. I could see Larry's shadow slumped on the living room couch. He would be dead to the world by now, passed out, done for the night. I looked ahead, to the right, to the left. It was late and nobody was around. Nobody. I was all alone, and I had survived.

Decision to Escape

My mind was racing. I had survived, but how much longer? How much longer before he killed me? I steeled myself, knowing I finally had to do something drastic. My life was on the line. At that moment, I resolved that somehow, someway, sometime, I would get the hell away from Larry. Whatever it took, however I had to do it, I would.

I became like a caged animal, watching for the one time when the keeper would forget to close the door. And only a few more bad episodes would occur before the opportunity came, to leave Larry for good.

One summer day—one sweltering, hundred-degree, humid and suffocating, typical South Texas day—I walked across the street to get a soda water. Now, I was a pretty good-looking woman with a nice figure, and, I liked to think, a pretty face as well. That's what had attracted Larry in the first place, wasn't it?

So it was hot, and by no means was I going out in pants and long sleeves. Instead, I put on short shorts and a T-shirt. Bra? Don't remember and it wouldn't have mattered, not with the shirt I had on, and the sweat-producing sun.

Did I want to be noticed? Yes. In all truth, I was tired of being beaten. I wanted someone to look at me and see a pretty woman. I wanted to hear a wolf whistle. I wanted to feel good about myself, at least for a few seconds.

And it happened. As I was coming out of the store, I heard a horn honk. Instinctively, I turned, wondering if there were an accident or something. Instead, it was just a bunch of guys in their twenties sitting in a convertible at the light.

"Hey, baby!" one called. "Mama mia!" shouted another. They were looking at me. Ogling. Wanting. And, for a moment, I felt great. As if I were beautiful. Honestly, I don't remember how I responded, whether I waved or smiled or just walked off without acknowledging them. In the end, it didn't matter. For the moment, I was Cinderella, but, this time, I was wearing the missing slipper.

Then all hell broke loose. I went into the house and was rounding the corner into the dining room when, suddenly, a fist shot out from behind the door, striking me in the face. I fell to the ground, dazed, wondering what had happened.

When I looked up, I saw Larry standing over me, a beer can in one hand and his eyes manic, bulging from their sockets. "I don't want to fucking see you waving to anyone else . . . or fucking talking to anyone else . . . and if I ever fucking see you going out in those shorts again, I'll fucking kill you! You got that?"

I heard him, but the words didn't register. I was too dazed, too confused.

"You fucking hear me?"

All I could do was nod. At least in the past, I had seen the abuse coming and could prepare for it. But this was something different. This had been an ambush. What was next? Killing me in my sleep?

I was sure another beating was coming, but, instead, he walked away. Just like that. Maybe he was too drunk, too tired, for a fight. Whatever the case, my resolve was getting firmer. I had to get out.

Where to Go?

But, still, there was nowhere to go.

At the time, I thought my parents were either clueless or just didn't care. Once, Larry had beat me when they were away, and it must have been really loud because, the next morning, they were knocking at the door. Evidently, the landlady had heard the screaming and called a forest ranger to track them down in the woods where they'd been camping.

"Oh, my God," my mother said when she saw my bruises. "What happened to you?"

"I fell, Mom."

She eyed me for several seconds, then continued, "It doesn't look like you fell." She tried to examine my body. "I don't see any scratches."

"They're on my back, Mom. I was going out to the garage, and I tripped and hit my head on the boat." That, I thought, was enough to explain my black eye.

Again, she looked at me skeptically. "Are you sure that's what happened?" she asked.

"Yes, Mom," I replied.

She asked me the same question again. And again. And, each time, I lied. I was so scared, scared she would find out what was going on, scared about how she would react.

Finally, she started toward the street, but then turned back. "One day you'll get your belly full of all this, and you'll want to come home. When you do, call me."

And that was it. Looking back, if I'd been her, I would have shot me full of tranquilizers and dragged James and me back to the house, thrown me in my room and locked the door, not letting me out until I gave my solemn word I would never, ever, go back. Why she and my father did not do this, I don't know. Maybe having been the one to go through it, I have a different perspective, but, if it were my daughter being beaten, I would have stopped at nothing to get her out of there, even if I had had to kill.

And killing was something I was increasingly thinking about. Maybe it was a cop-out, maybe it was my weakness, but I felt I had no other choice. And feeling that way is all that is important. I wanted out, wanted to run away, to take James and move to another planet. But spaceships had not been invented yet, and there was no colony on the moon to which to flee!

So, in my desperation, my thoughts turned to suicide and

murder. I fantasized about it, dreamed about it. I alternately thought of ways I could remove myself from this hell and/or take out Larry and free myself from his abuse. I was young, stupid, with no money and no skills. But, most of all, I had nowhere to go.

In my own way, I cried out for help, to my family and to others. Maybe I didn't cry out loud enough, or maybe they didn't hear me. I don't know. It doesn't matter now. It was what it was.

In retrospect, I wonder if maybe I should have gone to my parents and begged them for help. But the truth was I wanted—no, I *needed*—them to come to me. To take me away. To help me. Because I felt helpless. Helpless to do anything but suffer, to do anything but take it—and fantasize about a way out. Sounds pretty sick, huh? I know. But it was me, and the way it was.

You see, in those days, there was little help out there for battered women. There were no homes, no 1-800-Anonymous numbers, no support groups, no lifelines. There was just the abused woman who had to find her own way out.

When my mother left that day, I wanted to scream, to cry out, "Help me! Please, help me! He's going to kill me. Can't you see that? Can't you please, please, help me? I'm just a kid. Just a little girl. Help me!" And I was just a little girl, only fifteen at that point, so, after my mother got in the car, I fell to my knees and cried until I couldn't cry anymore. After I finished, I slept, right there by the door, until the sound of James's crying woke me up.

In more ways than one.

Finally Angry

Soon after, Larry was out partying with friends. I waited up as I usually did, but, this time, something was different. Instead of feeling sorry for myself, I was angry. Angry that all this crap had happened to me. Angry at my parents. Angry at the world. Angry at Larry. Angry that he had taken control of me and wouldn't let go.

But, most of all, I was angry at myself. For having let Larry do the things he did. For feeling stuck. For not doing anything. For being tired. For being weak. For being me!

Though I still wasn't prepared to walk out the door, I was "lucky" because Larry forced my hand. As usual, he came home late. I was watching television, ready to explode when he returned, ready to tell him he should be spending more time here, helping out with James and around the house. Then I saw him and the angry look in his eyes. I realized, too, that he was drunker than normal. And I knew, right away—this was it. This was going to be our final confrontation.

And one of us might not make it through alive.

He started in immediately. Seeing a cigarette butt in the ashtray, he accused me of having had someone over. "Who thhhe fuck wassss it?" he screamed, as he wobbled toward me. "Huh? Fucking telllll me!"

I looked at him, and, for the first time, saw him clearly as the monster and evil son of a bitch he was. "It's yours, Larry. From before you went out," I replied in a tired voice, then turned back to the television.

The next thing I knew, he had grabbed my hair and pulled me straight upward, almost ripping my scalp off. I screamed, but he didn't care. The fact is, he never cared. I was his trophy wife, his "bitch."

That night, I got the worst beating of my life. Punches, slaps, kicks, elbows—he threw whatever he felt like while I tried to resist, flailing at him with my arms and legs. Then he started dragging me around the room, by my arms, my legs, my hair. All the resolve I'd had earlier quickly faded. I pleaded with him, "Larry. Stop. Please, stop." I cried and cried and cried some more. I begged. But nothing worked. I was his to do with as he pleased.

When he pulled me upstairs, threw me on the bed, put his hands around my neck and squeezed, I thought it was over, that this was the end. "Oh, my God! I am going to die." I thought of all the things in my life I had done wrong, of all the people I would miss. Who was going to take care of James?

And, suddenly, I started fighting back again, flailing my arms and legs, trying to push Larry off as he continued to try to strangle me. But Larry was too strong.

I felt my strength dissipate, and I began to slip away. My mind became cloudy, as if someone had thrown a blanket over it. I couldn't think straight. I couldn't resist. I remember one thought: "I hope my parents don't have to see me like this." Then, just as I began to black out, it was over.

Larry had released his grip and I sat up, gasping for air, heaving back and forth, trying to breathe again. When I looked up and saw Larry, he was unbuttoning his pants. Within seconds, he was on top of me, pinning me down again on the bed. I had no fight left in me. I let him do his thing.

When he rolled over to sleep, I sat there and wondered what to do.

I was so frightened, I couldn't even sob. I was so tired, I couldn't even move. And I was so fed up that all I could think was, "I can't take this anymore." I looked down at Larry lying there, passed out, his chest rising and falling. I hated him then, with every bit of emotion I had. Slowly, I put out my hand and pushed his side, as hard as I could. He didn't even move. That's how drunk he was.

I sat there for a good ten minutes, my mind racing. What was I going to do? I almost died tonight. And what about next time? He was sure to kill me. It was just a matter of when. Would he kill James, too? I couldn't bear to think about it. So, I did what any normal mother would do if her child was threatened.

I resolved to kill Larry then and there, to save my baby and save myself.

Chapter 7

My Salvation, My Deliverance

I went into the bathroom and cleaned my blood off with a washcloth. I was cold, very cold, my body and my mind. When I was finished, I sat on the cool tile and listened to the quiet—eerily quiet—sounds of the night. I rocked back and forth for several minutes, knowing what I was about to do. Knowing the consequences but not caring. Knowing this was the only way.

Slowly, I lifted myself off the floor and walked quietly into the bedroom. I took one look at Larry sleeping there, half naked, disgusting, and knew I was doing the right thing. I opened the top drawer of the dresser, threw some clothes onto the floor, then found what I was looking for. Here was my salvation, my deliverance.

Shiny, black, and fully loaded, here was Larry's gun.

I hesitated only a moment, then reached in and cupped it in my hands. The metal was cold and I was shaking. I looked at the gun, then at Larry, then back at the gun. And I walked toward the bed.

My anxiety level was now rising as adrenaline pumped through my body. This was it. I was going to do it. I was going to escape. By killing Larry.

And I was no longer me, no longer Trudy Lynn. Instead, I was a killer. But it was all right. At this point, I knew it was him or me, kill or be killed. I moved toward "my husband" and felt a strange calming sensation overcome me. As if I were at peace. In heaven.

Larry was still passed out, lying there like the pathetic fool he was. I stood over him for several seconds, thinking only about how much I hated him for everything he had taken from me—my childhood, my life, and, most of all, my dreams.

In quiet anger, I extended the gun, placing the barrel only a few inches from his head. Then, I steeled myself and cocked the hammer. There was no turning back now. This was the end, one way or the other. No more beatings. No more cowering in fear. No more Larry. I was euphoric.

I put my finger on the trigger. Larry didn't move. Slowly, slowly, slowly, I started to pull it. I could feel the cold, inhuman metal. I looked at Larry one more time. Barely breathing, I said, "Goodbye," closed my eyes, continued to pull back on the trigger.

Then, in the quiet, I heard a baby's cry. James's cry. And I suddenly realized what I was doing. Oh, my God! What is going to happen to James if I kill Larry and go to jail? Who will feed him? Who will take care of him?

Shaking uncontrollably, I looked at the gun, shiny and black, and realized how close I had come not only to taking Larry's life, but also to ruining my son's and my own.

I had no idea how to disengage the hammer, so I ran down to the living room and set the gun on the table, then frantically began to pack stuff for James—formula, clothes, diapers—anything and everything that he needed.

Lifeline

Then I saw it. My true lifeline. The yellow phone with the rotary dial, shining brightly on the wall. I ran to it, pulled the receiver off the cradle, then stopped. What if Larry heard me dialing? What if he heard me talking? Quietly, I put the phone down. I couldn't take the risk of being discovered. I went to James's room, cradled him in my arms, then picked up the suitcase and the gun—still cocked—and ran outside toward the pay phone across the street.

As I ran, I was very conscious of the quiet. The street was empty. There were no cars, no people, no lights, no sound. I reached the phone and dropped the dime into the slot, as I held James, now sleeping again, in my other arm. Then I heard the brnnngg . . . brnnngg of the phone ringing on the other end.

And I waited, for what seemed an inordinate amount of time. It was probably only a few seconds before my father answered, but it felt like an hour as my mind raced. What if they weren't home? What if they'd gone on an unannounced vacation? What would I do then? Who would I call? I began to panic, breathing heavily, looking left and right, staring at the house, anticipating Larry coming running out the door any second. Then I heard a voice. "Hello?" my father said sleepily.

I have no recollection of what I said. What my father said. All I recall is, soon after, my father pulled up in the car, gently lifted the gun from my hand. and tucked me and James into the back seat. "It's okay," he said softly. "Larry won't hurt you anymore." I nodded, and he turned and slid into the driver's seat.

And I relaxed. For the first time in two years. Finally, I was safe. I held James more tightly than I had ever held him before, as, together, we fell asleep.

The nightmare was over. Or so I thought.

Hope and Reality

Most of the next few weeks are a blur in my memory. So much happened, so fast. My parents took James and me in, giving us not only shelter, but also hope. Soon, however, there was reality to deal with. I was fifteen-years-old, with no job, no money, no education, no guidance, and no prospects. What the hell was I going to do?

Not to mention that I lived in constant fear—the kind of fight-or-flight fear that gnaws at you, eats at you, persists no matter where you are or what time it is. Larry was a maniac, and I knew it was just a matter of time before he was going to find me and kill me. For weeks, I was afraid to go out of the house, and, when I did (because I had to go to work), I would lock all the car doors and roll up the windows, hide my face so that there was less chance that Larry would recognize me.

Still, when I went to the grocery store, Larry would follow me. "Slut!" he would scream from a distance. "I'm going to take the kid away from you, bitch." Waving a gun in the air, he continued his harassment. "If I can't have you, nobody is going to have you!" he would scream.

The only respite I had were the times he was away on oil rigs; then, for a short while, I could relax. But it was only a matter of a seven days or so, and then he would be back, following me, haunting me.

One time, I went to a party when I thought he was away. But he was not. Instead, he showed up with a high school girl, saw me, and started freaking out. When I saw him, I started to shake, and the other girls whisked me away to the bathroom as the guys there confronted him. Evidently, Larry was drunk and started doing his "karate thing." They threatened him and told him to get

72

his "wife beating ass the hell out of there." And he did.

Meanwhile, my parents meant well. They really did. And, I think, mostly they did good things when I returned home. My mother told me all I needed to do. Get a lawyer. Get custody of James. Get child support. "You need to get him to help pay your expenses," she kept telling me. At the time, I resented being told what to do, but, the fact is, I had no clue. I relied on them to make sure things got done, and, indeed, things did get done—despite the "stickiness" of the situation.

The Lawyer

You see, my parents were middle-class people, and that meant they had "status," "standing," in the community, as good, God-fearing Christians. I had already embarrassed them enough by getting pregnant at thirteen. Now I had to find an attorney and file for divorce because my husband was a wife beater. And going to an attorney meant the possibility of a trial. And a trial would be public record.

So, my parents did what they thought was right. They knew a lawyer who'd done some paperwork for them a few years earlier when they'd bought their house. They liked and trusted him, and, despite the fact that he was a real estate lawyer, my father persuaded him to take my case.

We went to his office on one of the hottest days on record, but, despite that, my mother insisted I dress "well" and that meant a dress and heels and all that—no shorts and a T. I remember being so nervous, I couldn't sit still. The fact was, I was going to have to tell someone all that had happened, and I had never told anyone, let alone some stranger.

So, we went up into this big, lavish office—carpeted and air-conditioned, with a huge sitting area and a receptionist with one of those fancy headsets. When we sat down in front of the lawyer's desk, he smiled at me. Warm and soft-spoken, he made me feel as at ease as he could under the circumstances.

My mother, however, did most of the talking. "He got her pregnant, then . . . ." She talked for a good fifteen minutes, but I had no idea what she said. I was in another world, half listening, half daydreaming. I didn't want to hear it. I didn't want to relive it. Instead, I kept picturing myself in my room, playing school with my animals.

Then, suddenly, I heard my mother's voice. "He beat her," she said. At that moment, my heart sank. For I knew I was going to have to talk about it. This was no nightmare, but very real, and something I would have to deal with.

The lawyer looked at me. "Is this true?"

I was paralyzed. My mind raced. What should I say? How could I admit this? It was all my fault. Not Larry's. I deserved it.

"Trudy?" he said again, still in that soft, kind voice. "Is this true?"

I couldn't look him in the eye. My gaze went around the room. To the plants. To the window. To the desk. Not to the lawyer.

"Answer the man," my mother said firmly.

I looked in the lawyer's direction, but kept my eyes focused on a picture behind him, a nice painting with lots of blues and reds. All I could do was nod slightly.

When I did, I sensed the air going out of everyone's lungs. I again drifted away as the lawyer turned back to my mother. Their voices continued above the hum of the air conditioner while I dreamed about my room and being a schoolteacher. About my animals. About being young again. About a world in which all this had never happened.

I heard only bits and pieces of their conversation. Child support, visitation rights, all the legal stuff. The lawyer asked more questions, about James, about the house, our possessions. And then I remember him saying something about possession being nine-tenths of the law. What did that mean? I must have looked quizzical, because he explained.

"Go back to the house when it's safe," he said, "and take everything. And, when I say everything, I mean everything that's paid for." I looked at him, then at my mother, then back at the lawyer. "Okay."

Paid For

When Larry headed out for a week, to work on an offshore oil rig, I made plans with my girlfriends—just some gals I hung around with when Larry was away or gave me "permission" (which was, in fact, rare)—and we went to the house, and, whew, if we didn't have a ball. They were also generally unlucky with men, and, together, we had one hell of a male-bashing bitchfest.

74

"Trudy," one called, holding a mug in her hand. "This paid for?" "Yep," I replied, and, quickly, she wrapped it in paper and threw it in a box. "How' bout this?" another called, displaying some cheap painting we'd gotten for the family room. "Yep," I said. Into a box, along with everything else that wasn't tied down, bolted to the floor, or otherwise couldn't be pried off the carpet.

The hardest part was going upstairs to get my clothes. I don't know how I did it. I tiptoed past James's old room and noticed the bedroom door was just a bit ajar. Suddenly, I couldn't catch my breath; I thought I was going to suffocate. What if Larry were in there? What if he'd come back early, or hadn't gone at all? What if he were just lying there drunk? What if, when I went in, I roused him out of sleep, and he'd realize what was happening, and kill me and all my friends?

I stood there for several minutes, listening for his breathing, or maybe a creak of the floorboards. But the only sounds I heard were those of my friends enjoying themselves downstairs, having fun and playing the good girlfriends.

Slowly, I tiptoed toward the door, then looked through the small crack. It was mid-afternoon, and the room was bright, but I could see only the corner and the window. Not the bed. Anxiety overcame me again. What if he were lying there passed out? What if . . . ? What if . . . ? What if . . . ? Again and again, I asked myself the question as I stood there, paralyzed by fear.

Then I heard one of my friends. She was laughing! Laughing so hard I could picture her doubling over on the couch. And I couldn't help but smile. With newfound courage, I opened the door with one push, and held my breath.

Nothing. No one. The bed was even made! By whom I don't know, 'cause I was quite sure Larry hadn't made a bed since his mother had forced him when he was seven.

I let out my breath, steadied myself, and walked into the room. What could I take? I marked the clothes, the smaller furniture, the lamps—again, everything that wasn't bolted down— then went into the bathroom to gather my toiletries, stuffing everything into a suitcase.

I started out the bedroom door, then stopped, turned, and looked back one more time.

This was the room. The room in which I had so often been raped, beaten, mentally tortured. This was the room within which I had experienced the worst years of my life. And I never wanted to see it again. Ever. "Go to hell," I said under my breath, then slammed the door behind me.

That bed? It was the only thing I left in the house.

Empty House

Downstairs, my friends were indeed enjoying themselves, throwing things around, asking "This Larry's?" when holding up some pitiful object. If I nodded, they'd shrug and throw it in a box, ready to go with us. I was going to take him for everything he owned, everything he had. I didn't care. Not after what he'd done to me. He was going to pay, and pay big.

We were all getting ready to leave when I realized I had forgotten one thing that had meant a lot to both Larry and me, though for different reasons. Larry liked to play music when he was drunk; I liked to dance when he wasn't around. And there it sat on the table—an all-in-one stereo console with eight-track player, silver and black with big jog dials for volume and tuning the radio, and black velvet-covered tinny speakers that put out just enough sound that you didn't have to strain yourself to hear. I just pointed, and one of my friends heaved it into her arms.

That was it. Damned if the house wasn't empty as the four of us packed up the stuff in the truck and headed home. It looked like someone had robbed it, and, in a way, I guess we had. But it was Larry, so, what the hell?

For a few minutes, I did stand by Larry's convertible. The lawyer had said to take it. It was paid for. But something stopped me. I still don't know what it was. Maybe it was because I was only fifteen and couldn't drive, but I don't think so. I think it was something deeper than that. This was Larry's baby, more precious to him than James or I ever had been. And it reeked of him. All over. The seats, the dash, the trunk. Sure, I could have sold it, but just the idea of touching it almost made me sick. I kicked it once— nothing big, a mere jolt with the side of my shoe—and then we were off.

Seeing Larry

For a little while, I did not see Larry at all. Then, one day, I was home alone with the baby. The front door was open, though the screen door was latched. I was busy doing something when I looked up and saw Larry there. I froze. I thought for sure he was there to kill me. Instead, as I looked at him, I saw that he seemed quite pathetic. He had been in a fight and had cuts over his eye and lip. He seemed so small. He told me not to be afraid, that he was there to apologize for all the things he had done. "I am sorry for the way I treated you. I'm quitting drinking and I'm gonna get some help. If you'll only come back with me, I'll treat you like a queen."

I do not know what went on in my head at that moment—only that I wanted so desperately for this nightmare to be over, I believed him. When he told me he wanted to come in—to see the baby—I agreed. When he came inside, he hugged me. I remained stiff, allowing him to hold me for a few seconds, but praying to God he would let go as soon as possible. Then I took him to the baby's room. James was sleeping, but I allowed Larry to poke his head in just to look.

James was on his stomach in his soft blue cotton onesie, his little bottom up in the air. The room smelled like baby powder—clean, fresh. The crib had been in our family for at least a couple of generations. It had those little round balls on top that made it look ornate and antique, and was situated by the window so James could feel the cooler breeze coming in on hot summer days. Larry looked in, then I quickly pulled him back into the hallway. He had seen James. That was the deal. A quick peek.

We were walking quietly down the hall when I heard a door close. Suddenly, my father appeared before us. I had never seen such an expression of intense anger; his eyes almost bulged out of his sockets when he saw Larry. "What the hell is going on?" he cried. "What the hell are you doing here?" he yelled at Larry.

Then, without waiting for an answer, he grabbed Larry by the arm and "escorted" him to the door. "I have a right to see my son!" Larry yelled as my father essentially threw him out onto the lawn. My father, though, would have none of it. "Get the hell out of here, and don't you ever come back," he screamed. "If you want to see your son, then you damn well better come back with the law, 'cause I'm not letting you near here again. You understand, you son of a bitch?"

Larry looked at me with plaintive eyes, but I just stood there thanking my father silently for doing what I felt I could not do.

That same night, I was out on the porch talking to a friend, when Larry drove his car by the house. Both my girlfriend and I saw him, and she tried to pull me inside as Larry came around again and stopped. "I'm getting the police," she said as Larry called my name. "I just want to talk," he said.

I looked at my friend and told her not to do anything—that I needed to talk to Larry. And I would have too, but, evidently, my father heard the ruckus and came out of the house. "Nell," he yelled to my mother, "call the law." Then he jumped into his big brown station wagon and chased Larry down the street. A few minutes later, he came back and told us that Larry had turned off his lights and given him the slip. When the police arrived, they went after him.

I am not sure what happened next. Did they find him, was he arrested, or had my father put "the fear" in his heart? Whatever, a short time later, I learned that Larry had gone off to San Antonio.

Free

I think I saw Larry only once more, at the divorce hearing, but I actually have very little memory of that event. For good reason. All I wanted to do was forget the previous two years. I think my mother was with me, and, of course, the lawyer. I remember thinking the judge looked old and mean. I said, "Yes, sir," a lot. That I remember. The lawyer whispered in my ear what to say and when to say it. Something about visitation rights. Child support. One hundred dollars a month. And then—just like that—it was over. The divorce was granted and I was free of Larry.

Free!

I was so relieved that, when I arrived home, I ran upstairs to get James, closed the door behind me, and just sat there cuddling him. "It's over, baby," I kept saying. "It's over."

And that was pretty much the end of Larry. We went to court one more time (he did not show), and the judge cited him for contempt and issued an arrest warrant. But I never heard one word more. Where he actually was, I didn't know, and, frankly, I didn't care. Sure, he owed child support, but tracking him down would have cost money, and my parents agreed it would be cheaper and better just to let him go and never have to deal with him again.

And I never did. Never saw him. Never heard from him. For all I know, he is long dead. Or maybe he won the lottery and is sitting on a beach somewhere in the Bahamas, living it up. If he is, I hope he gets a bad case of sun poisoning. Or maybe not. Heck, I don't care. He was out of my life forever.

Good riddance.

Chapter 8

Picking Up the Pieces

We all face times in our lives when things can go many different ways. We get out of a bad situation—a painful relationship, or maybe a job we can't stand, or a place to live we don't like—anything, really—and it's like starting anew, casting off everything from before and trying again.

I was now at one of those junctures. Divorced from Larry, free of his abuse, the world open to me—what was I going to do? Well, remember, I was still only in my teens. I was too young to get a driver's license, couldn't wait tables at a restaurant that served liquor. Heck, I couldn't even vote.

As I've said before, I had no money, no skills, no education. Just my parents and the help they were willing to give me. And I have to give them credit. They went out of their way to help, giving me food and shelter. I can't tell you how thankful I am I had that; I cannot imagine what I would have done if I couldn't have gone home. Lived in the streets? Maybe drugs or prostitution? What would have happened to James? I shudder as I think about what could have been. But, thankfully, none of that happened. At the very least, I had my basic needs met.

One of my parents' biggest worries was that James and I had no health insurance. If, God forbid, James got sick, doctors' bills could wipe out my parents' savings. So, they managed to tuck away their pride and allow me to get help.

I had a friend whose mother was a county welfare agent and a really nice woman. She brought me into her office, filled out all the paperwork, and got me on whatever assistance there was back then. Can't say whether it was Medicaid or welfare or what, but, every month, I received a check for $202, plus James and I had full medical, dental, and prescription drug coverage. I thought I was rich—202 bucks! I had never had more than twenty or so dollars in my pocket at any one time, and now? $202!

But, lest my girlish enthusiasm waste away hard-earned

taxpayers' money, my mother would always take it from me and put it in the bank. "Save it," she said. "You never know when you'll need it." (Thanks for the good advice, Mom!)

Okay, so I had a place to live, insurance, some money coming in. What next? Well, as my parents liked to remind me, they weren't going to be around forever, so they said, "It's time to get yourself a skill . . . time to see what it's like to be an adult."

At first, I was a little scared. Get a job? Work? Make a living? Take care of James on my own? But, the necessity of the moment dictated I put my fears aside and concentrate on what I wanted to do.

Part of me wanted to go back to regular school—math and history and all that. Yeah, I know a lot of you are saying "Yuck" right about now, but I missed it. I mean I really missed it. The angry teachers, hotter-than-hot classrooms, even the damned tests. I'd been in the seventh grade when I had gotten pregnant and I had liked school. Didn't always do so well, but I liked it. And, frankly, after what I'd gone through with Larry, school seemed very attractive.

But my parents insisted on my getting a job, and that meant the best I could hope for was vocational school. Well, my mother was a beautician, and I knew a lot of girls in the business, so it seemed only natural to enroll in beauty school.

First things first, though: I was too young to drive. So I applied for a hardship license, and, after six months of driving with my mother, I got it. I couldn't drive between sundown and sunrise until I turned eighteen, but at least I could get to and from school and work.

Beauty Boot Camp

So . . . beauty school! All I can say—and I apologize in advance for slipping into such overtly Texan vernacular—it was a hoot! I mean a liberating, exhilarating, spine-tingling adventure, from the day I enrolled to the day I graduated. One party after another. One good time after another.

Now, sure, some of you are saying, "Where's her sense of responsibility? She's got a kid! What's she doing partying?" Well, I have only one thing to say to that: give me a break. I was barely thirteen when I was raped, had a baby at fourteen, and then was beaten on a near-daily basis. I had never had a really good time—

you know, where you can let your hair down and enjoy yourself. I was, and still am, a good mother. I doted on James. But I NEEDED this. I had barely been outside my little town of Victoria. I needed an outlet. I needed friends. I needed some experiences. And so I make no excuses for the life I led during that period. Not a single one.

So there I was, a "beauty school teenager." I know the stereotype: the girls who go to beauty school are the dumb ones, the ones who can't hack real schoolwork. That's fine if you want to believe that, but I can tell you it was not that easy. Beauty school is just as serious as any other training. Your teachers work you hard. They make you study. And practice, practice. practice is their motto. Sounds just like any other profession, right?

And I also had a child to take care of.

Staying up nights with James, feeding him, cuddling him when he cried—well, it was a difficult time. I am not complaining. I was lucky to have what I had, to be alive, to have some help. Thankfully, my mother and grandmother took wonderful care of James when I was away at school or needed a night out with the girls.

So I worked my ass off. I had to learn everything from how to cut, to how to color, to how to layer. Heck, right now I sit on the board of directors of a nonprofit organization, but that's a piece of cake compared to beauty school. The teachers were harsh, and they never gave an inch. I joke about it now, but the girls and I used to call it "Beauty Boot Camp."

It's actually not unlike military training. You work from sunup to sundown. They drill you with exams, and get in your face when you're out of line. It may not have had the physical strenuousness of military boot camp, but the instructors had the mental part down pat. "Not good enough!" one trainer would shout. "Keep those hands up! Your technique is lousy." At the time, it was hard to hear those negative comments, but, in the end, I learned, and I learned because they were hard on us.

Yes, I learned, and, that, I have to say, was a good thing. For the first time in my life, I had learned something, a skill. And, if I kept up with it, I could have that skill for the rest of my life.

This was a real start, and I began to feel different. I knew I wasn't there yet, but it was beginning to sink in that I was going to be all right, I was going to be able to take care of myself and my son. And, for someone who had been through what I had been through, there could be no greater realization.

The Three Amigas

Just as important, I had made friends—real friends. These were girls who enjoyed hanging out with me, with whom I could joke around, and to whom I could tell secrets. You know, girl stuff. Real girl stuff! But that was exactly what I wanted . . . what I needed. Cathy and Johnna (so named because her father had wanted a boy . . . Texas—go figure!) were like sisters. They started school a little after me and graduated before (because I fell behind, taking care of James), but that was all right. We were like the Three Amigas. Carrying on, being loud, making our presence known, but, as I said before, having one hell of a good time.

And, of course, we did the normal school stuff, like practicing on each other—coloring, curling, cutting our hair, and trying new nail polish. We experimented with a lot of shag cuts with winged bangs. Heck, it was the '70s, and every girl in the world (at least, my world) wanted to look just like Farrah Fawcett (a native Texan, of course!).

We also shared the typical dramas—boyfriends and the like. But I relished every minute of it. I loved being a kid again, just enjoying myself.

We did do plenty of that. Our nights were spent at local dance halls, prancing around, flirting, the usual things. And drinking Mad Dog 20/20 with orange "sodie" water. That stuff was good. We'd go to Cathy's house first, try on each other's clothes, finally settle on what we were going to wear, and then we'd be off. (Of course, there were also the obligatory "cuts"—heading out of the shop at lunch and never going back. I think there were several times we caught hell, but . . . .)

One night, we ended up in Cathy's car, heading to San Antonio. Charlie Pride (a famous country singer at the time) was giving a concert, and, somehow or another, we had gotten tickets. My mother had said she would take care of James that night, and that I was free to go and enjoy myself. And so I did.

The whole car ride down, we were singing, laughing, dangling our legs out the window. Heck, we must have been a sight. But we finally arrived at the concert, along with thousands of other people, and danced and drank, and danced and drank some more, and had one heck of a great time. We made it back to

Victoria at three in the morning, but, somehow, still managed to get up for school the next day. I do remember I had one hell of a headache. But it was worth it!

Party Time

And then there was Cathy's wedding. Oh, my God! I had been brought up Church of Christ—you know—understated, simple. The only weddings I had attended were quick "I dos" and punch and cake in the church hall afterward.

But this . . . this was something to behold. Cathy was Catholic and her family was pretty well-off. I had never before stepped foot inside a Catholic church, and was it amazing! I mean, all those statues, the frosted colored windows, the decorations, the opulence. Yes, it was amazing!

I did the whole bridesmaid thing—rehearsal, rehearsal dinner, etc. And then the ceremony came, and the priest gave his sermon.

"It is a sin to have sex before marriage," he said, or something to that effect, and that was it. Cathy started bawling. The groomsmen were laughing themselves silly, and Johnna and I kept glancing at each other. Premarital sex a sin? Shoot, were we in trouble! Cathy did pull it together, said her piece, and that was it for the wedding part. Now came the reception.

As I said, I was from a small, very conservative family. My parents didn't like to make a big deal of anything, and, suddenly, there I was in the middle of a reception of two hundred people. There was a huge cake with a champagne fountain between each layer, a down-home Texas barbecue, a frigging band—a band!—and a huge dance floor.

Those of you from Texas know what I mean when I say it was one hell of a shindig, but, for those who have never experienced a real down-home Texas barbecue with all the trimmings, just imagine a bunch of oil men, cowboys, and fancily-dressed ladies whooping it up, not giving a damn about anything except having a good time, Texas-style. Well, that's exactly how I felt—amazed, exhilarated, enthralled. I don't remember any specific thing about the party, except that it was the best time I had had in my entire life. (And our reaction to the priest's sermon has given a good laugh for many years to those of us who stay in touch!)

Great Memories

So it was just me and James, and we were doing pretty well, if I may say so. For the first time in my life, I felt happy. I was doing something for myself, and only for myself. Going to school, working, taking care of my dear son. And, for a time, life was indeed wonderful.

I have great memories of those times. Maybe all of us do, who, after going through a difficult time, just let loose for awhile. I felt so free, so unencumbered. And there is nothing like that feeling.

I wish I could have captured it in a potion, and put it in one of those little bottles—you know, the kind with the perfume top, and you just open it up, and there are only a few ounces in there. But, just as with perfume, it would be enough, enough to bring back that same feeling.

Because, once again my life would change, and, once again, it would not be for the better.

Meeting Craig

Craig seemed like a really nice guy. They all do, and surely many of them stay that way, but, for some reason, I tended to attract the loonies. Or maybe it was the loonies who were attracted to me. Who knows?

Anyway, he was a handsome guy in his early twenties. Blonde hair, perfectly straight white teeth. Always wore Levi jeans, cowboy boots, and a T-shirt with a pack of Winston cigarettes rolled up in his sleeve.

Yeah, I know what you're thinking: loser! I should have seen it coming, right? Well, sure, now everyone knows you'd better be careful when you meet someone like that, because that kind of dress has become a cliché. But, back then, it was considered cool, at least by me and most of my friends. So, I can honestly say, I didn't know any better. But would I soon learn!

And, of course, I was attracted to him, and not just because of his looks, but because he drove a cool sports car. I can joke about this now, but that was my modus operandi, wasn't it? Good-looking guy with a fast car and I was hooked. To me that was the coolest thing in the world. God, I was so young!

We started dating. And, as I said, he was a good guy at first. We had fun together, he gave me money and presents, and, most important, he was good to James.

James was now two, and Craig would take care of him sometimes when I was in school or needed to run out for something. Several times I watched them together, and—I don't know—there is something about being a single mother and seeing a guy you are dating treating your son with grace and playfulness. And James loved Craig, loved playing with him and laughing together. To be honest, I was pretty much hooked at that point anyway. It was only a matter of time.

We dated for a year, the longest I had ever dated a guy, and we had a lot of good times. I knew Craig wasn't perfect, but who was? Who is?

Then, on New Year's Eve 1972, my sister was having a party at her house. I mean a down-home Texas party, serving whiskey and beer (none of that sissy wine stuff). And we were smashed, to the point where we were giggling incessantly.

So, when Craig took me into the bedroom and put me down on the bed, I laid there, looking up at the ceiling, my head falling to one side, and the room spinning around me. The walls actually seemed to be moving back and forth, back and forth. I felt like I was in an amusement park. Nothing seemed real.

Craig lay down next to me. His eyes were glazed over, but he wore an almost boyish grin. Then he said, all serious now, his tone low and urgent, "I want to ask you a question, and I want you to think hard because I will never ask you again." I remember wondering what the heck he was going to ask me, but, as I stared at him, his lips (moving in slow motion) and his words were not in synch.

"Are you ready?" he asked. I nodded, and he smiled tightly. "I want to know if you will marry me?"

Decisions

I can't tell if you if I was shocked or what, and I can't tell you how long it took me to respond, but, when I did, I burst out laughing. Uncontrollably. Just the way he was looking at me and the way he said it seemed so funny. I was still only sixteen, and had already been married to Larry—a nightmarish experience—and, the fact was, I did not trust men. Not any of them. As far as I could tell, they were only out for one thing, and you all know what that is. The last thing I wanted to do right then was get married

86

again.

But then I remembered he had said he wouldn't ask again, and I got scared. What if Craig was really the one? What if my fear was preventing me from seeing that? So, finally, I turned to him. He looked quite loving then, his eyes gazing into mine. And I said, "Yes."

We went back to the party and told everyone we were engaged. My sister toasted us; people congratulated us. All was pretty much rosy.

Later during the party, I was talking to another guy. I don't remember who it was or what were the circumstances of the conversation. Probably it was some friend of my sister's.

Craig, however, saw us talking and got mad. He came up to me, took me by the arm, and dragged me outside. He was pissed, and, when I say pissed, I mean his face was getting dark red. Then he took a whiskey bottle and threw it against the wall.

Here was another of those moments in our lives when we make choices, when our futures can go one way or another. Decisions made in those single moments can dictate a good portion of our lives.

And, in this decisive moment, I froze.

Literally froze, the cold biting at my body, into my flesh and bones. I couldn't move. What was happening? Was this Larry all over again? Or was it worse? Could it be worse? Or was it just a little jealousy, something I saw as very normal?

I was sixteen, and my whole life was ahead of me. In retrospect, I realize I should have run. Told him I was not going to marry him, and then run far, far away, to Houston, or Dallas, or some other big city where I could get lost and just go about my business and take care of James and maybe find a way to learn how to deal with my problems.

But this was small-town Texas, and, in my mind, there was still no escape and no one to turn to. So, when he calmed down, he took me to a hotel and we had sex. I can't say it was loving sex, since, at that time, I really didn't know what that was. Immediately afterward, I got sick. I don't know if it was the alcohol or the birth control pills or the psychological stress, but I puked my guts out.

Engaged

We were engaged for a year. I actually tried to break up with him a couple of times. The first time, he pulled a gun out of the glove box and stuck it to his head. "If you leave me, I'll kill myself," he said, cocking the hammer. Once more I froze, just sitting there watching him hold the gun to his temple, his veins throbbing. He was going to do it. He was really going to do it. How could I be responsible for that? He must really love me if he'd rather die than live without me. So I took it back. "I'll marry you," I told him.

Even as I said it, I knew I would try to find a way out. This was Larry all over again. How could this be happening? I had escaped it once, and now? Now I was falling down the same abyss, and, again, there seemed no one there to pull me out.

Craig had always drunk a lot, but that was pretty normal in the '70s. That's what people did, drank and partied. To be honest, there wasn't much else to do. Sure, we had a few movie theatres and a diner, but what was considered normal fun was to go out, kick back a few (or, in most cases, more than a few), and then cut loose.

Craig was definitely in the "more than a few" category, so, one night I told him he drank too much and that I couldn't marry another alcoholic. He cried and begged and told me how much he loved me. "Trudy, please," he whimpered as he got to his knees. "I love you so much. I'll do anything. Just please, please, marry me." In retrospect, I can see how pathetic he was, but, for some reason, I could not say no.

That was my problem in a nutshell, wasn't it? I could not say no to a man.

The only thing I insisted on was that we would not get married until I turned seventeen. I know it sounds bizarre, but, in my mind, if I waited, then somehow I would be an adult, and everything would be all right. I was still only sixteen when my mother took us down to the courthouse and signed for my license, but the wedding was set for July 6, the day after my seventeenth birthday.

Another Wedding Day

When the day arrived, my parents' house was filled with all sorts of beautiful flowers. There was a wonderfully decorated cake and pretty punch. James was wearing a really cute, blue, short pant suit. This time my parents were going to do it right, thinking, I guess, that this one would last.

I was up in my room getting dressed, and I could see out the window as the guests began arriving, everybody looking beautiful, the men in suits and the women in elegant dresses. Then Craig arrived, and, as I saw him come up the sidewalk and go into the house, I was suddenly gripped with fear. "Oh, my God! How can I do this?" Then I thought, "I can't do this! How am I going to get out of it?"

A few minutes later, my dad came up to my room. "Well, are you ready to go?" he asked.

I was wearing a wonderful, long, yellow dress—which I have to this day. I thought I looked pretty, like the perfect bride. But, as soon as he spoke, I knew I could not go through with this. How could I marry Craig and suffer for God-knew-how-long before I would again have to be saved?

My hands began to shake. I looked down, then up at my father. "No," I said resolutely. "I don't want to do this. I don't want to get married. I changed my mind. I am just going to jump out the bedroom window, and you go tell everybody that I decided not to get married because I don't want to."

I was such a child. I thought it would be so simple. Just run away and let my father handle it.

But my father didn't listen to me; he didn't hear the fear in my voice. He looked at me sternly, glowering, the way a father looks at a young girl doing something he considers irresponsible. His tone low and demanding, he said, "No, you can't do that. Everybody is already here. The justice of the peace is here. The guests are here. The family is here." Then, with a hint of anger in his tone, "Everyone went through all the trouble to make you a nice wedding, and you have to do it." Then he left.

My hands were still shaking. I did not want to marry Craig. I was looking for any way out, any way I could find. I had pinned all my hopes on my father, on his recognizing that this was not only something I did not want to do, but something I dreaded. But he hadn't.

Desperately, I looked around for some way out. I saw the window. I could have raised the glass, kicked out the screen, scrambled to the ground. I should have picked up James and run away, gone anywhere, just to get out of this marriage. It didn't even cross my mind that I could have gone outside, and, in front of everyone, said no to Craig. Or I could have called him up to my room to tell him I did not want to marry him. That's how helpless I felt. My father had been my only chance, and he had made it very clear he was not going to help me.

The "Appropriate" Thing

He came back a minute later. "It's time."

I lowered my eyes and mumbled, "Okay." Then, raising my head, "Will you walk out there with me?"

He looked at me for a second. He must have heard the plaintive tone in my voice, the desperate plea for him to help me through this. But he just shook his head. "Nope, you've got to do this on your own." And he turned and walked out of the room again.

My heart sank. My fate was sealed, and I was alone again, completely and utterly alone, isolated from my family, just as I had been with Larry.

Why did I feel this way? Well, I was still a child and I was weak. I had little education. I had no sense of the world around me other than what I knew in my little town. And, in that town, you did as your parents said.

Did they know Craig drank? Sure, they must have. Did they know I was afraid that Craig would turn out to be as frightening as Larry? They must have. But they couldn't very well tell all the guests they'd invited—the family, their friends—that Trudy had changed her mind, like some flaky little girl. But that's exactly who I was at the time. I was barely seventeen and knew absolutely nothing.

So, against my better judgment, I did the "appropriate" thing. I went outside. I got married.

I felt sick the entire ceremony, knowing my life was over, yet again. I wished I had that imaginary little perfume bottle with my beauty school life in it. But that was just fantasy. Reality was more of a nightmare.

Chapter 9

The Repeat Nightmare

To this day, I kick myself for not having the courage to run away from Craig.

I would have saved myself twenty years of pain, frustration, and anguish. Yes, I did get a wonderful daughter out of the marriage, but I was miserable. Beyond miserable.

I wonder what my life would have been like had I run away that New Year's Eve after he broke the bottle against the wall, or later, when he put the gun to his head, or the day of the wedding. But I didn't. I blame no one but myself. And I suffered the consequences.

The honeymoon was a tragedy in itself. We hadn't had enough sense to make a reservation in Galveston (right after the Fourth of July holiday), so we ended up driving all night to Houston to find a hotel room.

Eventually, we did settle into a nice hotel by the airport, nothing terribly fancy, but nice nonetheless. We were both pretty tired. It had been a long day and a long drive, but I guess Craig felt deserving of "honeymoon sex," and I felt obliged to provide it. No romance here. Just a quick "I love you," and we went to sleep.

The next morning was one of the weirdest I can ever remember. We went down to breakfast, and I remember things being very awkward. Looking back, I think I was in shock. What had I done? What was going to happen to me and James?

Was Craig thinking along similar lines? That he was only twenty-two and now had a wife and child to take care of, day after day after day, for the rest of his life?

We sat there, eating in silence for a good twenty minutes. I remember thinking, "I want to go home." I had rarely even been away from James overnight before, and the idea of being gone for two days had me worried. Typical separation anxiety, I know, but that didn't change the fact that I just wanted to go home and see my little boy.

When we were done eating, Craig and I really looked at each other for a moment, and then he said, "I don't know about you, but I'm kind of tired, and I just really want to go home now."

Immediately, I felt happy again. "Me, too!"

Living My Dream?

We went back to the room, packed up, and headed home, and it felt wonderful. All I had ever wanted was to have a nice home with a white picket fence, a loving husband, and happy, healthy children. That may sound "antiquated" in today's world, but that was my dream. Ozzie and Harriet . . . playing adult . . . moving out of my parents' house . . . setting up a home . . . being a housewife . . . cooking, cleaning, taking care of James . . . coming and going as I pleased—that was my DREAM!

We had bought a brand-new trailer home. (The house with the white picket fence was still a few years away. I hoped.) Yeah, I know what you're thinking—trailer park, alcohol, white trash, and all that. But I never saw it that way. To me, it was beautiful. Owning a home, even though small, was incredible. Our mortgage was only ninety-four dollars a month. We had a roof over our heads, food on the table. What more could I have wanted?

Still, the first year was hard, but not because of anything Craig did. I was homesick, crying pretty much every day. I missed having no responsibilities. I missed my mother. I missed feeling a sense of security. I was on an emotional roller coaster.

Anything could set me off—the noise of a crying baby from a neighbor's home or the sound of the phone ringing. I would hope and pray it was my mother calling to see how I was. Every day was like a minidrama. I never knew when or where I would break down, but I always did. Looking back, I guess I just didn't want to grow up, for whatever reason. And "playing" house had now turned into something real. It was all very scary.

For a while though, things with Craig were pretty good. Sure, I had to answer to him about where I was going and how much the groceries cost, but, for the most part, he was wonderful. He was great with James. He gave me plenty of money to do the things I wanted to do—go shopping, eat out, buy stuff for the house.

And he didn't care if I worked or not, so I did, a few hours a week in the beauty parlor at which my mother had worked.

Mostly, I took care of older women who came in once a week to get a shampoo and set. Remember, it was the '70s, and, in Texas, big hair was in—and it had to hold until the next week. So we're talking rollers, lots of hair teasing, and tons—and I mean tons—of hair spray in big ass bottles filled with all those nasty CFCs that supposedly destroy the ozone layer. I would spray and spray and spray until the woman's hair was fixed and firm, just like concrete. A stone thrown at it would probably have hit with a thud and bounced off. That's using hair spray!

Life with Craig

I won't go into all the gory details of my relationship with Craig, as I did with Larry, but I think it is important to give some idea of what happened so you can understand what led me to the decisions I later made.

Basically, Craig eventually turned out to be an asshole—a mean-spirited, alcoholic jerk. Although he never hit me, he scared the crap out of me several times. But he was not a wife beater. And, though the emotional and verbal abuse was terrible, I always pointed to the fact that he did not slap or punch me as a positive. Yes, I was fooling myself. But, at the same time, coming out of the experience I had had with Larry, this was a step in the right direction . . . or so I thought.

As I said earlier, Craig was a drinker, but I thought that was normal. He was in the oil business and out in the field most of the day, and I guess I rationalized all the drinking by saying to myself he had to blow off steam somehow. It was hot out there, over one hundred degrees in the summer. Working around heavy machinery that spewed all types of hot gasses into the air, these were rugged men, guys who liked to talk trash and live hard, who thought they deserved to let loose and run wild.

I can't remember the first time he cheated on me, but there were many. One time, when he hadn't come home by midnight, I called one of my friends and we went out looking for him.

Found him in a beer joint, sitting on a barstool next to a barmaid. Damned if I didn't fly off the handle. I was pissed. Beyond pissed. He was my husband. What the hell was he doing with another woman?

I stood there for several seconds, then looked around. One of several pool tables in the joint wasn't being used. I grabbed a cue stick off the felt, swung it around, and smacked Craig clear off the barstool. Drunk, or maybe in shock that I'd done that, he just stood up and got back on his seat, like nothing had happened.

Later, I found out he was having an affair with that woman. If I'd known, I would have smacked her, too. And suffered the consequences, jail or whatever. I didn't care. That's how pissed I was.

It would have been a crime of passion, of rage and jealousy and everything in between. A crime committed in the name of love. What's the old proverb? "Hell hath no fury like a woman scorned"? That was me at that moment. I was ready to trade eternal damnation for another chance to whack them both over the head with that pool cue.

Another horrible event occurred during one of the many times we were separated. Our daughter was then only a year old, James just a few years older. I was in an apartment, rented from someone I knew, when I got a phone call from a friend. "Craig was by here," she whispered. "He's drunk as hell, carrying a loaded gun, and he's looking for you."

I freaked, literally freaked. I gathered up the kids, went to another friend's house, and called the police. I gave them a description of Craig and his pickup, and they pulled him over, handcuffing him on the spot for drinking and driving.

"Where's the gun, sir?" they asked, and then he knew I had turned him in. He went to jail, but his boss came down and bailed him out. Buddies knew buddies who knew the DA, so he was never convicted on the weapons charge. (After all, this was Texas, where the good ole boy system was not only alive and well, but where it was invented!)

The Children

I spent more than twenty years with Craig. We had our daughter, Sherry, together, and he helped raise James. But you want to know the worst thing about living with an alcoholic? I kept telling myself I could take the emotional and verbal abuse; I was used to it. But I saw how it affected my children.

Once, I had them in the car when I picked up Craig at a beer joint. He was so drunk, he was puking all over the place. I had to stop the car God knows how many times so he could get out and throw up, all while the kids watched in horror.

And there was the night when Craig was so pissed off that he threw me up against the wall, then kicked an ice chest at me after I landed on the floor in tears. I literally picked my daughter up out of the bed in the middle of the night and told James to get in the car. The next day was his sixteenth birthday, and he had to hide in a hotel from his father. And Sherry? She was nine, living in fear day after day.

I cannot tell you how much guilt I have to this day about those twenty years, about how I kept us there. I tried to leave— eight, ten times, probably more?—but, each time, Craig promised things would change, that he wouldn't drink, the affairs would end. And, like an idiot, I went back, each and every time.

He was suicidal for much of our marriage. One time, he cut up his arms and threatened to run through the glass door. I tackled him and wrestled him to the ground. Another time, he came home with a loaded rifle and threatened to blow his brains out. So there we were, fighting for control of a loaded gun. Hell, both of us could have been killed. Where would that have left the children?

For many women, it may be hard to imagine things getting this bad and not walking away. But that's how it is. Those of us who have been so abused and feel so trapped—we become desperate. I know I lost all sense of reasoning. None of it seemed real. It was all like some terrible nightmare—a repeat nightmare, in my case. And I did feel trapped, like the walls were pressing in on me, and I couldn't move, couldn't escape.

Drama followed drama, day after day, like the day he shot off the rifle and I thought for sure he had killed himself. Or the day I came back from my sister's in Houston, where I had fled, to file papers for divorce. I got a call saying Craig had shot himself in the chest. He wasn't dead, just bleeding, and had made it to his brother's house before passing out. The ambulance took him to the hospital, and his family begged me to take him back.

So I did. Again and again. Until, finally—as my mother always said, "You'll leave when you get your belly full of it"—I was full of it.

Turning the Corner

This time we were again separated, but he came out to the house for something. He was in an alcoholic stupor, drinking so much by this time—a case of beer a day—he'd been diagnosed with neuropathy.

This meant the alcohol had damaged his brain so much that neurons were no longer making connections correctly from his brain to his legs. He could barely walk straight, even when sober. They used to call it "wet brain."

I started telling him he would be in a wheelchair for the rest of his life with nobody around to take care of him, that he was drinking himself to death and would die a lonely, crippled old man.

We were outside and both the children were there. Young adults by this time, they had watched the meltdown between Craig and me day after day, year after year. Now he was screaming at the top of his lungs, calling me every name in the book. "You're a bitch! You're the one that's crazy! It's your fault I turned out the way I did!"

Then he kicked dirt on my legs and spit his gum out at me. To me, that was the worst thing he ever did, worse than cheating on me, worse than drinking and screaming, worse than the time he had thrown me against the wall. And, right then, I made my decision. I thought, "I've got to leave town or I'll never get away from him, I'll never be free, I'll never be happy. I'll never experience peace and quiet unless I leave."

So I packed up my stuff, rented a U-Haul, and drove away. I remember thinking as I headed out of town, "I'll never go back. This is it. I'm never going back."

The first week in Austin was like a wonderful dream. I felt like I had that potion with me, and I'd been able to take a sip and just float away for a little while. For the first time since I was a child, I went to bed feeling completely safe, knowing nobody could threaten me, nobody could hurt me, that I could sleep and dream and wake up and make myself coffee and relax and just enjoy life.

And knowing that somehow, some way, I had turned a corner. I could do anything I needed to do—on my own. And I was sure I would find redemption.

Chapter 10

Redemption

Now for the rest of the story of how the abuse I've recounted affected my life beyond just the immediate physical and emotional scarring. All these experiences, in the end, made me stronger —made me who I am today. And many people helped me along the way. So very many loving and kind people served as lampposts in an otherwise dark world. Many of them, to this day, continue to give me hope.

Hope. Redemption.

Bob Marley's "Redemption Song" is a beautiful call for freedom and peace. Yes, he was talking about slavery. Yes, he was talking about the journey of African-Americans. But it is a powerful song about all kinds of freedom and, of course, redemption.

I had struggled for so long to find some sense of balance in my life; a way to help myself and, thus, help others; a sense of purpose; and a belief that I could do more than what I'd managed until that point.

In my mind, through that struggle has come my redemption.

Hidden Abuse

When I married Larry and, later, Craig, I knew of no other battered women. As far as I was aware, there had never been another emotionally-abused woman or a wife raped by her husband.

The Burning Bed—the 1980 book by Faith McNulty and the 1984 TV-movie starring Farrah Fawcett—brought such horrors to the forefront of the American consciousness, and now, heck, they're in the news every day. Hundreds of books have been written on the subject; there are support groups for battered women, and even a clinical diagnosis—Battered Woman

Syndrome. Courts which once immediately would have sent a woman to jail for doing harm to an abusive husband, are now recognizing the pathologies behind the actions, and some women are granted clemency.

Now I am not condoning violence, in any form, and the work I do tries to prevent situations from ever getting close to that point. But, back in my day, that sometimes seemed the only choice for women. Where could I have gone? A shelter? In little Victoria? Ha! Maybe in Houston or Austin or Dallas, but they were hundreds of miles distant, and what did I know anyway? I was thirteen-years-old when I got married the first time.

I had always had a strong personality. Yes, I had been beaten and abused, but, through it all, I had wanted to get out, to find a way. But there were no hands reaching out for me, or, at least, none that I saw. I'm not sure how many years Craig and I had been married before I determined I had to do something. If I couldn't help myself right then, I decided I was damned sure eventually going to try to help others, to keep them from going through the same things I had.

As most often happens in life, though, I did not have a "eureka" moment. No epiphany on a summer night staring at the stars, no light bulbs flashing on, no lightning bolts striking. Just a series of failures and accompanying accidents.

The Quick Fix

One of the times I left Craig (and I really don't remember how many there were, but it was a big number), I moved back in with my parents. Despite all that had happened earlier, they were very good to me once I had decided to "get a life" for myself. They helped with the kids, making sure they were fed and clothed and cared for. And, of course, I didn't have to pay rent. All that gave me some time to try to figure out what I wanted to do.

The series of failures at that task—that ultimately led me to success in counseling and social services—began with real estate school. I had a friend going, and she asked if I wanted to join her. "Sure," I said naïvely. "Sounds great!"

Of course, with little more than an elementary school education, I had no idea how hard it was going to be just doing simple math, but, the fact was, to get in, you didn't need a high school diploma, or any other education for that matter. I just signed my name, paid the fee, and I was enrolled. Sounds good, right? Well, not so much.

I labored through the class and sat for the board exam. It wasn't pretty. I no longer remember my score, but it was bad. So, I took it again, and, lo and behold, I passed! Although I had studied my ass off, nobody was more surprised than I was.

Nevertheless, I had indeed managed to get my license, and I started selling real estate. However, I wasn't very good at it. Not because I couldn't handle the hours or the work, but because I hated it. I mean, I understand some people love schmoozing and making small talk, but it was definitely not for me! Within a couple of months, I had quit and gone back to work in a beauty shop.

See, the problem with my life was I was always looking for a quick fix, always trying to find that one thing that would make my life perfect, right now. It took me a long time to figure out that, well, life isn't perfect, no matter how hard you try to make it so. In fact, the harder you try, the less perfect it becomes, or so it seemed to work for me.

For Their Sake and Mine

During these years that I was going back and forth between Craig and my parents or friends or apartments, I started volunteering at a women's crisis center in Victoria. In the beginning, I just talked to women on the phone and, occasionally, in person, mostly trying to give them the courage to walk away from bad relationships.

Sometimes it was as simple as a five-minute call to say, "You can do it. You really can." Other times, the conversations were long and involved, lasting an hour or more, often with no resolution. I couldn't help everybody.

And my dirty little secret those days was that I couldn't even help myself.

To be honest, despite the encouragement and advice I was giving others, I wasn't sure I could handle walking away.

Others who have been through something like I went through, whatever the specifics of the trauma, should be able to identify with the feelings of guilt and shame that come up no matter how hard you try. You start reliving experiences while you're on the phone or when you're talking to someone, and it takes a great deal of discipline and experience to shut those things out—to clear your mind of all the things that happened to YOU, and to focus on the other person.

It's not easy, but, once you find yourself in a good mental place, it's amazing how much you can feel true empathy for another human being—amazing and scary at the same time. You place all your needs in the background and focus solely on the person you are trying to help. And, once you're there, you're there. You've got it!

As I said, it took time for me to get to that place, and, every once in awhile, I still feel a little twinge in the back of my mind. There are just some experiences you cannot forget. You can resolve them, but you can't "un-remember," and smells and sights have a way of bringing images of those times to the forefront of your consciousness no matter how hard you try to keep them out.

One day in particular I will never forget. I'd been working at the crisis center for a short time, and I was sitting at my desk doing some paperwork when, suddenly, I heard tires screech and a bloodcurdling scream—the kind that is a manifestation of primal fear.

Alarmed, I jumped out of my seat. Was it a car accident? A murder? My God, what had happened? Several of us rushed toward the door at the same time, and found, outside our little green house in the middle of a residential area, a woman lying in the street, bleeding all over.

Somebody went inside and dialed 911 while two of us went to help her. She looked badly beaten, bruised in many places, and not just from ending up on the street. She was crying, trying to form words, but her lips were trembling, and we couldn't understand.

We knelt beside her, stroked her hair, and told her an ambulance was on its way. Before it arrived, she was able to sit up and tell us who she was. As soon as she did, we remembered her.

She had called our hotline two, maybe three, days earlier, looking for a way out. Her husband had been abusing her and, from the looks of it, severely. When he found out she had called us, he beat her some more, threw her in the car, and drove to our office, pushing her out onto the street, barely slowing down as he did so.

We were able to get her into the ambulance and on her way to the hospital where they would take care of her physical wounds. Later, we would take care of her emotional ones.

I felt anger that day, anger like you can't imagine. How could one human being do this to another human being? It didn't make sense. And you may wonder why I would stay there, day after day, volunteering mostly, not getting paid. But I tell you, if you had gone through the things I had, and you knew you could help others at the same time you were helping yourself, you'd find you really didn't have a choice.

I don't mean to get into ideas of free will or anything, and, certainly, I could have moved to Hawaii, found a place on the beach, and worked odd jobs to support myself. But that was not me.

Remember, it was the late 1970s when domestic abuse was barely a blip on the radar (especially in small-town Texas). We were doing pioneering work in South Texas. Yes, it was hard. Yes, it was sometimes traumatic. But we were doing something important. And I felt good about myself. I was making a difference in other women's lives. For the first time in my life, I had a sense of purpose, something that made me get out of bed in the morning, saying, "I can't wait to go to work!" I was not perfect. I still had problems, but I was getting myself together. I was making a living and building up my self-esteem. And that's all that mattered.

Not All That They Seemed

After a bit of time as a volunteer, I started a paid position, counseling violence victims, drug addicts, and alcoholics. But things were not all that they seemed. In fact, I was not well mentally. I won't share all the gory details, but I must admit I tried suicide several times—some halfhearted and some full-out, honest to God, attempts.

This is probably the best example in the world of someone stating the patently obvious, but, the fact is, I survived! And, now that I look back on it, I can't believe I had gotten to that point and had ever acted on my thoughts.

One time, I decided to asphyxiate myself. I put the car in the garage, closed the door, then ran into the bathroom to check my makeup, adding a bit of lipstick and a little more eye shadow. Heaven forbid I'd be caught dead looking frightful! Then I went to my room to get my childhood Bible. If I was going to kill myself, I was going to need to ask God to forgive me.

That all done, I went back to the car, started it up, rolled down the windows, and leaned back, clutching the Bible against my chest. Craig would come home in a little while and find me unconscious. Dead. Gone. Free.

However, after a few minutes, I heard a moan, a whimper. I opened up the car door to find the family dog. "Oh, my God," I thought. "I'm going to kill the kids' dog. They can't lose their mother and their dog in the same day." So, I jumped out of the car, opened the little doggy door to let him out, then headed back to the car to finish what I had started.

But the phone rang, and, without thinking, I went into the house and answered it. The caller was my sister, a counselor at the time. I told her what I was doing and she quickly talked me out of it. I had to go back and turn off the car, then I finished talking with my sister, thinking the whole time, "Okay, not today, but soon. Soon."

Getting Help

I had started seeing a counselor right around then. Jay had actually been a teenaged friend of my son, and had gone into social work. Talk about weird! But he was a good man, a nice man, someone I could talk to about my problems, especially a way I had found to help me "cope" with my life—prescription drug abuse. He worked for the Palmer Drug Abuse Program (PDAP), a nonprofit that didn't charge me. (If they had, I would never have been able to afford it.)

PDAP had some very strange philosophies, or so it seemed to me. A lot of their counseling took place standing or sitting in a circle, holding hands. That kind of touchy-feely stuff scared the crap out of me. But the primary purpose of PDAP was to bring love and understanding to others in order to promote healing, and, were it not for them, their love, their support, I doubt I would have made it. The truth is, that organization saved my life. (It also saved the life of my son.)

So, there I was, one cold day in December—somewhere right around an anniversary of the first "incident" with Larry—talking with Bob, the senior counselor. He was telling me how they all loved me, how they all wanted me to get better, to be healthy and happy. He was sitting in a chair right next to me, trying to hold my hand as he spoke, but I refused to let him. Instead, I sat there thinking how God-awful this whole "therapy" experience was. You see, in my universe, all men wanted was sex. So I was skeptical, to say the least.

I was very depressed at the time, and had been contemplating suicide for awhile. I was taking antidepressants, pain killers, tranquilizers, and muscle relaxers prescribed by my family physician. I was not taking care of myself. I was dirty. I wasn't eating. I wanted to die. The pain was so great that I just wanted it to stop.

And I was paranoid. I had terrible nightmares in which I was running, running for my life. I would turn around and see Larry chasing me, a beer in one hand and a knife in the other. I kept running, but Larry always gained on me. Every step I took, he took three. Every moment he was getting closer, closer, closer, then . . . .

Suddenly I would wake up breathing hard and in a cold sweat, wondering if I were still alive. I would look at my hands, turning them over just to make sure they were still there. I turned this way and that and looked under the bed, to make sure no one else was in the room.

Maybe I was safe, but I certainly didn't feel that way. I was an animal, running, hiding, still trying to escape my past. I just wanted everything to stop. All of it.

Plan B

Then, one day, I told Bob everything. Told him about my "Plan B" if the counseling didn't work, or if things got too tough. The fact was, I trusted him, more than any other person I had ever met. He was good to me . . . good to everyone. . . kind, compassionate. And real.

That day, Jay had escorted me into Bob's office and waited with me for "the chief" to arrive. When he did, the three of us sat in the small room with wood-paneled walls and a floor that crackled. (The clinic was two portable silver buildings alongside each other, and they swayed with the wind.) When I first was going there, I kept thinking how ratty a place it was, how it was "beneath" me. But, the fact is, it was a great place—a healing place—and it was there I found the most comfort.

Bob started telling me how the medication I was taking

was bad for me, and that I should stop as soon as possible in order to clear my head for counseling.

They knew! They knew! My dirty secret. They were going to take my pills—my pills!—away. What would I do without my only crutch?

Bob looked at my purse and nodded. "I'll bet you carry them in there," he said.

I looked at him, shocked. "How did you know?" I asked.

He just smiled. "Can I see them?"

I hesitated for a moment, but, damn Bob! He was so nice! I took the bottles of pills out of my purse and handed them over, afraid he was going to throw them in the trash. In fact, I was sure he would. Or down the drain. Or something God-awful like that.

He kept telling me to trust him. "It's okay, Trudy," he said. "You can trust me. You can." But I didn't feel that way. The last people I had trusted? My girlfriends in beauty school, and that had been a long time before.

But I gave the pills to him and that was that. That was the start of me getting better.

Stopping the Pain

Two days before, I had given up. I had been feeling hopeless for a long time, just knowing that life could never get any better. I still carried the pain, the fear, from my time with Larry, and now I was with Craig. Day after day, night after night, I was being terrorized by my own mind. And, though I had children, I truly thought they would be better off without me, their crazy lunatic of a mother.

So I had planned it all. One day, when everyone was out, I would hang myself on the patio. Craig came home every day at the exact same time, and he would arrive and find me—dead. He would know, and I wanted him to know. He could tell the children something else . . . that there had been an accident . . . anything, but he had to know what had really happened.

Sick, huh? Yes. But I had been dealing with him for years, and I wanted him to suffer as much as I had suffered. So there. I've said it. That's the truth. And, the fact is, I wasn't able to think clearly about the effect on my children because I was so desperate, I *knew* they would be better off without me. At least I kept telling myself that.

And, when the moment comes, you're not thinking of anything else besides pulling the trigger, jumping off the chair, swallowing the bottle of pills, cutting yourself to pieces. You're on autopilot, a zombie. You're already dead. You just haven't made the transition from being a walking, breathing creature to one six feet under.

So, no more crying. No more prayers: God, take care of the kids and forgive me for what I am about to do. It's simply where you are at that moment. And that is where I was.

I rigged up one of Craig's leather belts (the ones he so loved!) on the rafter and put a chair underneath. It was a beautiful day, the sun shining, the pasture across from our house peaceful, the cows slumbering through the afternoon. Everything was so quiet, so very quiet. I could feel the breeze on my face, could smell the fresh-cut grass. I thought back to when I was a child, and the cool air that used to waft over me when I was on the swing chair. Swinging would be nice. Did I have time for one last swing? Just one? No. Craig would be home soon. And I had to "take care of business."

It was a good day to die. In fact, it was a great day to die.

I climbed up on the chair and stood on my tiptoes. Made sure the belt would hold. Looked out once more at the cows, anger now filling me. "You deal with this, Craig!" Then I placed the belt noose around my neck and tightened it as much as I could. Slipped the buckle in place, then took one more look at the pasture. "'Bye," I whispered to no one.

Then, kicking away the chair, I fell toward the ground, ready for whatever God had in store for me.

I wasn't prepared, however, for the jolt my neck took without breaking. The next thing I knew, Craig was screaming, grabbing me. "Oh, my God, Trudy. Oh my, God, no! No!"

He stood there holding me as I watched from some dreamland. Supporting me with his shoulders, he took out his pocketknife, cut the belt in two, and caught me in his arms. Threw me in the pickup and drove me to the hospital.

Now, two days later, there I was with Bob and Jay. Bob had dumped my pills in his hands. "You see these, Trudy?" he began. "There are people who would kill you over these, would melt them down and shoot them into their arms. Do you want to die? I mean, do you *really* want to die? Or do you just want to stop the pain?"

Killing Secrets

I didn't even know that was a possibility. So I looked at him, hoping, praying. His gaze was so kind. And all I wanted to do was cry. For the first time in my life, I realized what a serious situation I was in—how close to death I really was. Bob and Jay told me they loved me and they would help me. They told me they didn't want me to die. They told me of a place out in Arizona where I could go to get help, a treatment center in the desert. And, the next thing I knew, I was being escorted to the airport in Houston.

One of the best moves I ever made.

My suicide attempts were another of my family's dirty little secrets. And, if there is one thing I've learned in life, it's that secrets kill. They kill you, they kill others around you, and they usually do so slowly and painfully.

I learned that in the drug treatment center in Arizona. I'd been there for several weeks but was making no progress. One day, Mark, my counselor, confronted me in group. "Trudy," he said, "you're not doing well and I think it's because you have a secret or are holding something back."

Immediately, I began crying. Indeed, I did have a secret. I couldn't take it anymore, not the drugs, the abuse, the depression, but I had a backup plan. I had hidden Craig's old straight razor underneath the eye shadow tray in my compact. If this treatment didn't work, if I didn't get better, I had my way out.

Now, however, I told Mark and he sent a nurse to check. The nurse found the razor, went through the rest of my stuff again, and that was it. My backup plan was dead.

Funny though, as soon as I admitted that, I started getting better. I started talking more, opening up, enjoying myself. The point is, secrets make you sick. Doesn't matter how big or how small. If you give up your secrets, you get better. If you don't, you die—one way or the other.

Education

To be quite honest, suicide had seemed the only way out . of my situation, but, now that I had been to treatment and started talking about my situation, I had less inclination to die. That continued despite the fact that, when I returned home feeling pretty good and ready for a fresh start, I found out Craig had been sleeping with my best friend while I was away.

But I dealt with it, and, over the years, as I left and went back to him numerous times, somehow I found my strengths. And, despite having only an elementary education, I kept going back to school.

Besides finishing beauty school and obtaining my real estate license, I also earned drug abuse counselor intern status from the State of Texas and a Social Work Associate license. Later, I would be grandfathered in as a Licensed Bachelor Social Worker. I became the executive director of two nonprofits before I had even received my GED. All the while, I couldn't even spell "executive." In fact, I had a little cheat sheet with the words "Executive Director" spelled out. That way, when I had to sign my name and title, I was sure to get it right.

I can laugh about it now, but it is hard to express how scared I was that I would be found out. I used to have terrible dreams in which I'd be sitting in a boardroom, giving a presentation. Suddenly, someone with an angry, judgmental expression would point at me and scream, "Fraud! Fraud! She's a fraud!" I would protest my innocence, but the man or woman would look at the others and say, "Watch," then turn back and challenge me: "Spell this . . . spell that." I would sit dumbfounded for several minutes while the others stared and waited for my response. I would open my mouth as if to try, but then would sink back into my chair. "They've found out! They've found out!" And then I would wake up in a cold sweat, alone and afraid.

My real experiences were often just as embarrassing. At conferences and other professional get-togethers, I'd hear, "What school did you graduate from? I went to 'so and so' and just loved it." I would smile politely and make some excuse, all the while panicking on the inside. "Oh, I'm sorry. I have to use the ladies' room. I'll be back in a second," I would say. Or I would pretend I didn't hear the question. Over the years, my excuses became a sort of art form, as I created an "out" for every conceivable situation.

Still, however, it haunted me. I felt less than equal among all those highly educated people. No matter how many women I helped or how much "success" I enjoyed, I was still very insecure about having dropped out of school in the seventh grade, about never attending college.

New Challenges

But, despite my fears and anxieties, despite my lack of education, I persevered, working my way to redemption as a crisis hotline volunteer, as a program director, as an executive director. And each new "title" brought new challenges.

As a hotline volunteer, I started dealing more and more with rape victims. I went to the hospital with them and held their hands as nurses removed their clothes to be analyzed and bagged for evidence. I saw women's eyes fill with tears and, above all, fear of what was going to happen next—a fear I knew well. So, I tried to make it just a little better. You'd be surprised how even something as small as having replacement dresses available in all different sizes can make the situation a bit more bearable for a rape victim. At least they'd be able to leave the hospital with some shred of dignity intact.

I also helped train new police officers. (Later I was to receive a Citizen's Merit award from the Victoria Police Department for my work with the officers.) I was the "victim"—a woman who had just been raped—in a role-playing exercise. And, frankly, it was horrifying. Dressed in a gown and made-up with fake bruises or whatever, I would lie on a makeshift hospital bed while rookies tried to deal with me.

Many were so poorly trained they just had no idea what to do or say. When, in my role, I told one I wanted to die because my husband was a gambling addict, he started by telling me that a little gambling was okay even though gambling was illegal in Texas. Another talked about his wife's instability, and yet another ran out screaming, "I don't need this bullshit!"

The fact is, these officers were not bad men; they just did not know how to deal with a woman in this situation. Used to being around men most of their lives, they had little experience dealing with women other than their wives in ANY situation. That's just the way it was back then.

Luckily, that has changed over the years. More women are now involved in the process, and they and the men have been trained and tested, and trained and tested again. These people are not shocked to come across a rape victim or suicidal woman. They've been there. They know how to deal with the situation. And that makes all the difference.

One of the proudest accomplishments of my career has

been our Children's Center, primarily because it was the community which funded it. All kinds of men and women poured out their hearts to create a place where children could be children. Instead of the gray office suite in which our staff had previously worked with kids, we now had a "playhouse" full of colors and toys and stuffed animals, a TV and VCR and tapes.

While we talked with their mothers or aunts or other caregivers, they could forget about the outside world for awhile, about the violence they endured or witnessed at home. They could just laugh and play and be. Over the years, it has continued to grow, and now includes an advocacy center. To this day, our Children's Center still receives community support.

Ending the Cycle

I could tell you more horror stories that would make you cringe, but I won't. Instead, let me emphasize that, if my message about domestic violence boils down to anything, it is that the community must take an active role in making life better for the women and children who have suffered and continue to suffer.

That's the way the cycle can end. That's the way daughters of abused women do not repeat their mother's horrors, and sons do not grow up to be abusers themselves.

Sometimes I wonder what my life would have been like if, when I was younger, there had been the type of support system available there is now. To be honest, I don't know if I would have reached out. Maybe I would have . . . maybe not. But I do know this: many women and children *are* helped by the efforts of these community outreach programs. From California to New York, from Alaska to Hawaii, and around the world, for many women, these programs are lifesavers in every sense of the word, and I am proud to have played my role.

I'm proud, too, that I've continued my education. Five years ago, I enrolled in a college degree program, going to school mostly at night and doing much of my homework on weekends. I know it may not seem like much to those of you who went to college and graduated as a matter of course. But, for me, that day when I receive my degree, when it comes—and it will come—will be joyous!

Earlier, I told how I made excuses when someone brought up the subject of college. In fact, I know now it doesn't really matter because my experience far outweighs anything I will ever learn in a classroom. But, still, my degree will be a personal accomplishment—an achievement on the same scale to me as the moon shot was to the engineers of NASA!

But my role has not simply been that of counselor and student. I have continued to be lover, friend, mother, and daughter.

Although Craig and I now have been apart for ten years, I still have some contact with him; he is very sick with alcohol-related illnesses. I visit my daughter and son as much as I can, and they are both doing quite well for themselves, despite what they went though as children. I go to family barbecues and visit with my father and mother and sister and aunt and cousins. In essence, I *live*—something I did not do for a good thirty years.

Life isn't perfect. But it's my life. And that's just how I like it!

Epilogue

Redemption Revisited

Redemption. What a lovely word.

Redemption. Say it a few times. Doesn't it roll off your tongue, leaving a taste of something sweet in your mouth, as if it were a piece of candy?

Redemption. Surely it means different things to different people, so I can define it only for myself. You may not agree with my definition, but I ask that you look at it from my perspective.

The word conjures up so many images in my mind, images of pain and healing, of being belittled and being encouraged, of finding hope where there was once only despair. Redemption is not a destination but a journey, and the path is not a solitary one. For me, it started when I opened up and allowed myself to be helped, when I began trusting others and taking steps—sometimes small ones; other times, large leaps—into the unknown. And it began with knowing that, if I fell, there were those who would help me back onto my feet.

So many people along the way:

- a hotline volunteer who helped me develop a safety plan to leave Craig;
- a stranger who cast a kind look in my direction as I walked, despondent, down the street;
- a friend who slipped some money for food or clothing or a movie into my pocket, without saying a word and without any semblance of judging;
- a man who told me he loved me without conditioning his love on my giving him sex;
- a teacher who gave me a hug;
- a boss who understood when I desperately needed a day off just to get my head straight;
- a community college dean who bent the rules and allowed me to take an English class when I had not

fulfilled any of the prerequisites;

- a GED instructor who encouraged me with kind words, and instilled in me a sense that I could indeed do anything to which I set my mind.

And the cancer patient who refused to give up hope, even when all hope had seemingly vanished. Who battled and battled through the pain, through the suffering, without ever once complaining, "Why me?" That woman was my cousin, and she died very recently. I am so sad, but I take heart that she was prepared and she was at peace. I will always remember her for her courage, and for her sense of humor through her ordeal.

Of course, I also have been inspired by women I've counseled out of bad situations, then encountered years later with smiles on their faces where before there had been tears. What can be more heartening than meeting these women again after they have accomplished goals they once thought impossible?

To Be Happy

Redemption. It's about a reawakening, about coming out of a crucible not only alive, but with a sense of purpose, with a feeling of well-being, with an awareness of all the wonders life has to offer. It is about rebuilding bridges which had been all but washed out, about finding some peace with the past, about being able to move forward in life. It's Bob Marley, it's Trudy Lynn, it's you—it's all of us.

You know, I once truly believed I was destined to be unhappy, that happiness just wasn't my lot in life. For a long time, I kept buying into that, convincing myself it was true. Then I did things that made it true, surrounded myself with people who made it true. It's like the chicken and the egg. You believe something, so you make it happen, so you believe it some more, so it happens some more. I never was good at physics; in fact, I've barely heard of Einstein. But this definitely sounds like something he would recognize as a crazy force in this universe.

But frankly, folks, those long-ago thoughts were, and are, a bunch of crap.

EVERYONE has the right to be happy. In fact, I might go so far as to say, everyone has a DUTY to be happy. It's not easy for many of us. I am certainly a testament to that. Some people do have it easier than others, born into it with a great family, great parents, a world of opportunities, and hope from the very day they come into this world.

Some of us, though, have to struggle our way there, struggle to find that lighted path. We suffer, we cry, we pray and we pray, we cry, and we suffer some more. Then, one day, we just wake up. "My life doesn't have to be this way," we say. "I don't want it to be this way," we say. "I can be happy."

Possibilities

And, suddenly, life changes. You start opening your eyes and seeing the world as a lovely place no matter how many bad things are going on. You start finding the good in everything. You start meeting nice people. You start feeling better even about yourself. And, just like that vicious circle of pain and suffering, you end up in a "vicious" circle of happiness! Suddenly, what before seemed impossible is now not only possible, but happening.

Your life before seems like a dream (or, more accurately, a nightmare), and you now find yourself in an alien world where strange things happen. People smile at you. You have good friends who treat you well. Good things happen as a matter of course.

All you can do then is smile and laugh and think back to the way things used to be. "I was so blind," we say, "blind because it seemed so hard, like there was this insurmountable wall I could never climb." Even at my worse, I had known the wall was there, and I had pined to get over it. I just knew there was something special on the other side, filled with hope and love. But I was scared, scared even to look at the wall, much less try to climb it. I was scared to see what was really on the other side, scared to pick myself up and do what was necessary to get there.

I would take two steps toward the wall, then one step back . . . three steps forward, two steps back. It wasn't always pleasant facing that wall each day, but now I know it was worth it. When I finally scaled the behemoth—when I finally said, "To hell with this life of hell!" and I took that first step upwards—there was no turning back.

That first step is the most difficult. But, once you take it, things start to get better, and quickly. Everything seems possible. Hard, yes. About that I will not lie. But possible.

And isn't that what it's all about? Possibilities?

113

Personal Note

Some might read this book and say I have been cursed. That my life has been nothing but a series of horrors, repeating themselves again and again. Sure, I've had some tough times. But how can I look at where I have been and where I am NOW, and not say my life has been full? Of ups and downs and, of course, plateaus, but is that not what life is? A journey that is sometimes thrilling, sometimes scary, sometimes painful, and sometimes joyful? If so, then indeed, I can say I have lived!

Maybe God meant my life to be like this. Maybe it was part of some "Big Plan." I really cannot say. It is strange, but, now as I reflect on my past, I cannot help but think of God. Many years ago, only a few years after marrying Craig, I was "saved." It was a strange moment for me because I didn't feel saved—not before and certainly not after. I was twenty, and there I was sitting outside the church, waiting for the time to go in and proclaim my belief in Jesus. I had smoked. I had drunk. I had fornicated. In truth, I was a mess. And there I was sitting, and all I could think about was that I didn't want to go to Hell.

Finally, they called me up the aisle, and the preacher asked me if I believed Jesus had died to save us. "Yes," I replied, as my mind swirled with doubts and fears, hopes and dreams. "Do you accept the Lord Jesus as your Lord and Savior?" the masculine voice asked. My head still swirling, again I answered, "Yes." As the preacher nodded, the choir started to sing "Amazing Grace."

I don't care what religion you are, or what your beliefs are, but that song has something magical to it. Something that transcends any one particular faith or belief. And there I was, standing at the front of the church, as the choir sang:

Amazing Grace, how sweet the sound
That saved a wretch like me.
I once was lost, but now am found,
Was blind, but now I see.

That first verse really got to me. My eyes started watering. I saw myself as the "wretch." And I felt so happy that now I would be going to Heaven. That I wouldn't be left behind in Hell. The next Sunday, I was baptized.

Not Giving Up on God

Maybe that should have been enough to change my life forever, but it wasn't. I don't consider myself an "unfaithful" person. In fact, at this point in my life, I very much believe in God. It's just that my attitudes have changed. Where before, I had done things or not done things out of fear of going to Hell or of being left behind, now I do things because I want to. Because being a good person and making the world a better place are fundamental to the teachings of Christ and any other religion.

Today, I believe God is a loving God. That he wants good things for me and for others. I still seek guidance and strength and courage, and I still pray. For my family, for friends. I am very thankful for what I have now, for peace of mind, happiness, a loving family, a place to live, and plenty of food.

Some of the teachings from my childhood years are still fundamental to my beliefs. Asking forgiveness for my sins, not lying, not talking bad about people, not cursing, going to church regularly. I'm not perfect. I sometimes slip up, cursing here and there or not making it to church, but, in the end, I think I have evolved. I no longer fear God, but I embrace him as a source of well-being. I work to make my life and the lives of those around me better, and I try to be a good person. Maybe everything does happen for a reason. (I'm just not privy to it!)

I never gave up on God, even through the difficult times. I may have been angry, despondent, wondering why all this crap was happening to me, but never once did I give up. Even when I tried committing suicide, I believed God would forgive me, despite what I had been taught. That he would understand my pain and that he would see to it that I found my way into Heaven.

Not Giving Up on Love

And never once did I give up on love either. Even when things seemed hopeless, there was always that romantic notion that, someday, I would find someone who would love me. Who would treat me well. I cannot say I know romantic love in a deep and tender way, but I can say I have loved. I didn't know it at the time, but, after years of experience, I am quite sure that it was indeed love. And no, it was not Larry. And it was not Craig.

Many years ago, after I had divorced Larry, my sister was dating a young man, and, one night, he and his cousin came over to our house. I will not mention the cousin's name here, but he was a good, kind man, well-kept, attractive in a mature and sophisticated way, soft-spoken, with dark hair, and eyes that sparkled with a sense that he knew something nobody else did.

Immediately, we hit it off, and the four of us went to a country dance hall. Now, I did not know the first thing about real dancing; I just kind of moved with the music. But this man spent the entire night showing me steps and encouraging me to learn, and he did so with patience and kindness. It was like heaven being in his arms. He was the first man to treat me like a lady—to treat me with respect and sincerity.

He loved James and treated him, as far as I could tell, as he would his own son—in a more mature and fatherly manner than Craig would later. His family was open and kind, accepting me and James as if a teenaged mother were nothing to be concerned about. We went together for a good amount of time. I played cards with him and his family, went out to nice restaurants, shopped at nice stores where he bought me a long beautiful dress and James a red velvet outfit. All in all, I enjoyed every minute, and, for the first time in my life, I felt feminine—like a true lady.

He told me he loved me very early on, but, in my experience, men had used the word "love" capriciously, saying it only to get into your pants. But, that whole year, he never tried to sleep with me. Never did anything that might have set off my warning signals. And, one night, something happened which might have led me down quite a different path.

We were drinking a little bit, and we went to park on a country road. Things got a little heated, and we ended up being naked and about to have sexual relations. As we did, however, something in my head popped. This was the first time I had even seen a naked man since Larry, and I just about freaked out. I started pushing on his shoulders—pushing him off me. "Stop! Stop! Please! Stop!" I cried, tears running down my cheeks. I couldn't go through this again. I just couldn't.

And, in that brief second after I had screamed, I started to shake. Would he stop? Or would I be raped yet again? But he did stop. And the look of kindness and concern on his face as he buttoned himself up and took me in his arms was the most genuine expression I had ever experienced in a relationship. "Baby, I'm so sorry. I'm so sorry. I would never do anything to hurt you. I love you." And then he held me and held me and held me as the tears continued to flow. "Shhh . . ." he said softly, "everything will be okay," as he rocked me gently in his arms.

I will never forget that night. The way he spoke. "Everything will be okay." Soft, loving. Words that have meaning even today. When I think of him saying that to me, my eyes well up with tears.

Unfortunately, I was too young and too screwed up at the time to recognize what a good thing we had. How much he truly loved me. And, when he found out I was dating someone else as well, he told me he wanted a committed relationship or nothing. I think his exact words were, "I won't play second fiddle to anyone." He wanted to marry me. He wanted to take care of me. He wanted to be with me for the rest of his life. But I was not ready for that. I was not ready for a mature, adult relationship. And he left quite upset.

A few days later, I received my first box of roses. Pink, if I recall—wonderful, beautiful roses. The card read, "Everything will be okay." It takes a special man to walk away understanding that the girl he loves is not ready for him. It takes an even more special man to write the note he did, knowing that he would probably never see me again.

Closure

As the '80s came, my life had taken a new turn. I was in Corpus Christi at real estate school, and this man had become a police officer there, and had a wife and children. I used to drive by the station on my way to class, and, every time, I felt my stomach tie up in knots. It was so painful, still with Craig and dreading it, knowing how my life could have been so different if I had been ready all those years before.

Then, one day, on the spur of the moment, I stopped at the station and wrote a little note on my business card. "Everything will be OK." I signed it and left it with the duty officer. I went on to class, not thinking about the note since I had not really said where I would be. About halfway through the session, someone came up to me and said there was an emergency and I needed to go to the front door. I just about panicked. What had happened? I jumped out of my seat and ran out of the room down the hall.

And there he was. Standing tall, handsome as ever, a large smile on his face. I couldn't believe it. How had he found me? I ran toward him, and, as he opened the door, I jumped into his arms and he swung me around as we kissed for what seemed like an eternity. It was wonderful to be in his arms again, to feel his cheek against mine.

"I called your office and they told me you'd be here," he said. "I was so happy to get your note." We went to a little café and talked, then took a walk on the beach. It was one of those perfect nights. Warm with a slight breeze, the stars bright in the sky. Like a dream—some perfect fantasy.

He told me about his family. I told him as little about my life as I could. He asked me if everything was all right—why I had left that note? He thought something might be wrong. I told him, "No, I just needed closure." After fifteen years of wondering, I just wanted to see him one more time. And to tell him that I had loved him all these years despite the both of us being married, and I was sorry for the way I had treated him.

As I spoke, he stopped, turned toward me and took my hands in his. Looking at me with those kind, loving eyes, he said, "I wish you would have known that fifteen years ago," he said, without a hint of bitterness. He was about to say something else, but I stopped him. "It's okay," I said. "I don't expect anything from you now. I know you are an honorable man and committed to your wife and children. It's just, well, I wanted to see you one more time and tell you this." He nodded and smiled.

We walked some more, and then he took me back to the café and to my car. As I slid into the driver's seat, he kissed me one more time. Neither of us spoke, but, as he closed the door, our eyes met again. As he drove off in one direction, I in the other, all that was going through my mind was that indeed I had known love, and it was truly wonderful. It did not matter I was not with him. All that mattered was that this moment had been real, and that was all I needed.

I still think about him occasionally. Still fantasize that we'll meet up again in old age and live happily ever after. I know that's not very realistic, but, if it's not him, I hope it is someone very similar who steals my heart. Someone as kind, as loving, as decent and honest. Even today, I find myself daydreaming about him, and, when I do, I know I deserve to be loved. And that is the most important thing.

Friends and Family

And indeed I have been loved by many. All I have to do is look around at the friends and family who have stood by me all these years, and I know I've been lucky to have these people in my life.

These people have given me their support when times were good AND bad. They have never asked me for anything other than my friendship. They have made me roll with laughter and given me their shoulders on which to cry. They have shared their lives—their sorrows and their joys, their doubts and their dreams.

And then there's my sister, who I absolutely hated for a time as a child, but who has been there for me every day and every moment of my adult life. She has given her time, her energy, her caring, and her love.

Most of all, I just have to look at my children—my beautiful, thoughtful, loving children—and I feel an overwhelming sense of joy.

If I ever start to question the threads of my life—what could have been—the questions stop right there: with my children. My son and daughter gave me their love, their support, their friendship, despite all the things I put them through. Never once did they give up on me. Never once did they blame me for their situation. They have always given me their understanding and their dedication. And for that I am so very thankful.

I love them dearly, more dearly than I can express here, for words cannot describe my tears, cannot capture my heart fluttering as I write, cannot begin to explain the depth and breadth of my emotions. But I will try anyway, because, if anyone deserves these last words, it is they.

So to you, my son and my daughter, thank you for standing by me all these years; thank you for the smiles and the laughter; thank you for the joy you have brought into my life.

Thank you, thank you, thank you. You are indeed my jewels and I love you both very deeply.

Your mother,
Trudy